WHICH? WAY TO GET AN eLIFE

About the authors

Carol Elston and Sue Orrell own and run a successful IT training and development business in Leeds. They have written many IT textbooks which are used within schools and businesses.

Acknowledgements

A lot of very knowledgeable people have helped in the preparation of this book. The authors and publishers would especially like to thank Sean Blessitt, June Bromsgrove, John Bromsgrove, Mark Elston, Cliff Redford, June Redford and Mark Taylor.

Anna Alston, Imogen Clout, Jonquil Lowe, Elizabeth Martyn, Sian Morrissey and Richard Wentk also contributed to the book. A number of people at Consumers' Association helped ensure the accuracy and reliability of the information in the book.

WHICH? WAY TO GET AN eLIFE

Carol Elston & Sue Orrell

 CONSUMERS' ASSOCIATION

Which? Books are commissioned by
Consumers' Association and published by
Which? Ltd, 2 Marylebone Road, London NW1 4DF
Email: books@which.net

Distributed by The Penguin Group:
Penguin Books Ltd, 80 Strand, London WC2R 0RL

First edition January 2004

Copyright © 2004 Which? Ltd

British Library Cataloguing in Publication Data
A catalogue record for *Which? Way to Get an eLife* is available from the British Library

ISBN 0 85202 939 X

For a full list of Which? books, please call 0800 252100, access our website at www.which.net, or write to Which? Books, Freepost, PO Box 44, Hertford SG14 1SH.

Editorial and production: Joanna Bregosz, Nithya Rae
Index: Marie Lorimer
Original cover concept by Sarah Harmer
Cover photograph: Frank Whitney/gettyimages

Typeset by Saxon Graphics Ltd, Derby
Printed and bound in Wales by Creative Print and Design

Contents

Introduction

What exactly is an elife and why should you want one? An elife is a life that includes the use of the Internet. And the main reason you might want to consider getting an elife is to improve the quality of your existence by saving time and money, and in many cases reducing stress.

Everyone can benefit from something the Internet has to offer: be it information, advice or services. You may well have heard the cliché about being able to shop in your pyjamas – well, it's true. You can also access your bank account in the middle of the night; chat online with a friend thousands of miles away; and book a holiday or car hire without leaving the house. And, most importantly, you don't need to be a computer whizz to make it happen.

One of the best things about the Internet is its flexibility: you can use it as frequently as it suits you, you can choose what activities to do electronically and in real time, and you can decide what aspects of it will best enhance your lifestyle. Clearly, not everyone would enjoy buying clothes over the Net, and many people like to smell and feel fruit and vegetables before buying them, but there are tasks that are routine or are hard to accomplish without a lot of time at one's disposal, and this is where the Internet comes in handy. Even if you are reluctant to complete the task online, you can still take the pain out of some of the legwork. Treat the Internet like any new tool – test is out, take it slowly and when you have mastered it you may find that there is no stopping you.

Since the early 1990s the Internet has changed the economy and our lives in a number of ways.

The Internet is shaping the way we **communicate** both within our own community and worldwide. Facilities such as email, instant messaging, video conferencing, text messaging and chatrooms have opened up an exciting range of communication channels. These innovations have revolutionised the speed of communication but have also introduced new challenges and safety issues, particularly with respect to the young and vulnerable.

The **buying and selling** of commodities and services online has changed the world of commerce significantly. We now have a worldwide, open market and easy access to information, especially on the costs of things. This has helped empower us as consumers because we can compare prices and deals and make choices based on that information.

Tasks such as banking online, buying financial services and seeking legal and business advice are still in their infancy. **Managing our finances** online is one area of the Internet that has been slow to lift off, but it is only a matter of time before more of us take it in our stride.

The Internet has it all as far as **media, leisure and entertainment** go: Internet radio, MP3 music, online TV programmes and movies, news and weather reports, sports information, online gambling, hobby clubs, facilities for booking tickets for the theatre, cinema and sporting events, and so much more. This is one area many people have embraced, and the variety of services is sure to increase.

Despite the fact that the Internet brings us millions of websites, in the UK we tend to play safe and stick with what we know and trust. A survey by BT Openworld found that sites hosted by high street stalwarts such as Marks & Spencer and WH Smith are more trusted than the online bookshop Amazon, one of the most famous web brands in the world. The report also revealed that the BBC has the most trusted website in the country. This book should inspire you to try out some lesser-known sites.

You will find sites that you like and want to revisit but equally you will find sites that are frustrating, have appalling customer service and are best avoided – in fact, just like shopping in the high street! This book shows how to access the best sites and avoid the duds.

Which? Way to Get an eLife explores the many downsides of the Internet too: the presence of misleading, objectionable and wrong information on less-than-reliable sites, safety concerns and security issues, among others. It helps you steer clear of unsavoury material and shows you how best to achieve your tasks.

Have an open mind and give it a go. You may even find you get hooked. And if you do, and the Internet is taking over your life, don't worry. There is even an Internet addiction site to help you with this (www.netaddiction.com). Happy and fruitful surfing!

Chapter 1

The Internet

It is amazing how quickly the Internet has eased its way into everyday life. Even as recently as the early 1990s, few people outside of academic, research and government establishments had heard of the Internet. Today, it is estimated that about 30 million people in the UK and 600 million worldwide use it to search for information and send emails.

This chapter starts with some basics: it explains what the Internet is and what it can be used for. If you are a casual surfer or are relatively new to the Internet, this chapter will go some way towards demystifying the Internet for you.

Personal computers

Although computers have been around for some time, their shape and size have evolved over time. In the past, they were typically large, cumbersome beasts primarily used by companies to process large quantities of information (*data*).

The home PC market

It wasn't until around the mid-1970s that powerful compact computers came into circulation. Small enough to sit on a desktop at home or work and powerful enough to carry out the tasks of the individual business or home user, they became known as personal computers or *PCs*. The upsurge in the sales of home PCs can be largely attributed to increased competition among computer manufacturers. In recent years, powerful and sophisticated technology has been introduced and all at a much more affordable price than previously. The obvious uses of the Internet, such as the ability to search for information and send digital photographs across the world, have captured the imagination of the public at large and have been instrumental in turning the PC from a luxury item into more of an essential commodity.

The Internet

The Internet began in the USA in the late 1960s. It is a common myth that it was created as an information network that could survive a nuclear attack. In fact, the purpose of the original project was simply to create a robust network – the ability of the Internet to survive a serious attack has been greatly exaggerated. What remains true though is that the Internet's designers realised that their network could be used by anyone, with almost any kind of computer.

And so today the Internet (often called the *Net* for short) is a huge worldwide network of computers linked together. No longer the prerogative of American researchers and academics but extended to individual people all around the world, the Internet provides us with the means to communicate with each other and share information.

Your PC on the Net

So, how does your individual PC at home fit into the wider picture? One PC on its own is referred to as a *stand-alone PC*. If you create information on a stand-alone PC you will typically save it on to a fixed or *hard disk* inside the computer. The only way in which you can share this information with another PC user (if it were not for the Internet) is by giving him or her a copy on a floppy disk or CDROM – a stand-alone PC has no physical link to any other PC and sharing information is not all that easy.

Lots of businesses link their computers together (using cables, optical fibre or wireless connections) so that employees can share information with each other on a *network*. Networks often include large, powerful computers known as servers that are used as libraries of facts and software. The Internet is based on the same principle. It is an extensive network that incorporates individual and networked computers all over the world, all linked together by a huge system of cables, telephone lines, satellite links, wireless radio connections and servers. So instead of copying a file on to a disk to give to someone, you could send it by email (see Chapter 5).

Linking to the outside world

There are several ways of getting on to the Internet. Your PC can link to the outside world via your home telephone line. In many parts of the UK you can also use a satellite dish or a radio connection. If you use a laptop PC, you can also connect to the Internet over a mobile phone. (To learn more about connecting to the Internet, see *Connecting to the Internet* later in this chapter.)

What can the Internet do for you?

The Internet has become hugely popular among people of all ages. It has opened up a whole new world of live entertainment, online shopping and instant communications via chat rooms, discussion groups and email.

The Net and the Web

The Internet has always been a vehicle for sharing information but until quite recently much of the material on it was plain text interlaced with programming codes. It was not presented in a way that many of us would have easily understood, let alone felt inspired to take a closer look at. However, in 1989 Tim Berners-Lee, working at a physics laboratory in Switzerland, had the idea of making documents available on the Internet for other physicists to share. He came up with the idea of linking pages of information together so that it would be easy to select a link and jump to a document of particular interest. It wasn't long before companies began making software to present these pages, and the links between them, in a visually appealing way. And so began the World Wide Web.

Put simply, the World Wide Web is the most accessible part of the Internet. It is an extensive network of interlinked pages packed full of all sorts of exciting information. Today, these pages typically contain multimedia material – text, pictures, sound files, video and animation – all designed to attract and hold our interest.

11

Among other things, you can use the Internet to:

- keep in touch with friends and family around the world via email
- take part in news and discussion groups (known collectively as Usenet)
- transfer files such as free software from large digital warehouses to your PC
- get the latest news, sometimes before it appears on TV and radio
- access the billions of pages of information which make up the World Wide Web
- research your favourite interests
- search for and find bargains
- create and share your own web pages to show photos and share hobbies or perhaps to promote a small business.

Who owns the Internet?

No one owns the Internet as such. Companies that provide cables and computers which link into the wider network are responsible for maintaining their own sections of the physical network. A number of organisations, most notably the Internet Corporation for Assigned Names and Numbers (ICANN), administer ownership of the Internet's equivalent of street addresses, known as domain names (see Chapter 2). Otherwise, groups and individuals that provide services or post information on the Net are responsible for keeping their own services and information up to date.

Who puts information on to the Internet?

Anyone can put information on the Internet and so billions of pages of information are available. The nature of the content is incredibly diverse: you can find all sorts of things ranging from mainstream up-to-the-minute news, travel and weather reports through to coverage of minority topics that to many will seem offensive or even downright bizarre. This can make surfing the Net a fascinating, addictive and frustrating pastime.

However, this strength of the Internet – that anyone can publish material on it – is also its main weakness. The quality of the information on it clearly cannot be guaranteed. Despite obvious concerns about the nature of some of the material published, however, most Western governments do not find it cost effective to police or filter all the information that is available. Many organisations adhere to strict codes of conduct about what and how they publish, and their services may regularly come under the close scrutiny of industry watchdogs. Many other sources of material, however, go unmonitored and unregulated.

Connecting to the Internet

Connecting to the Internet is known as going *online*. Although the majority of people still do this using an ordinary telephone line and a modem, new ways of connecting to the Internet are rapidly evolving. Speedy hi-tech connections using broadband technology are becoming more readily available, as are connections via satellite, cable TV, mobile phones and other hand-held devices.

To connect your PC to the Internet you will generally need:

- a PC with software that enables an Internet connection (but see *Accessing the Internet without a PC*, below, for alternatives)
- a telephone line
- a modem
- an account with an Internet Service Provider (a company that will connect you to the Internet, see below).

Dial-up modems

Most people connect to the Internet via a dial-up modem, which enables information to be sent from one computer to another down a standard telephone line. As most households already have a telephone line installed, this is a relatively cheap and easy way to access the Internet.

What is a modem?

Because computers and telephone lines do not generally speak the same language, a special piece of equipment called a *modem* is needed to get the two to talk to each other. Computers store information as a sequence of digits 1 and 0 (digital format) and this needs to be converted into electrical voltages (analogue format) before it can travel down the telephone line. It then needs to be converted back into digital format at the other end so that the receiving computer can read it. Most computers these days come with a built-in modem as standard. If yours does not, you can buy a modem to plug into your PC for less than £50.

Modems are capable of transmitting information at different speeds (kilobits per second) depending upon their specification. You should buy a modem that will give you a speed of at least 56Kbps and which conforms to the International Telecommunications Union standard known as V.90 (most recent modems do).

Theoretically, the greater the number of kilobits per second, the faster the speed at which your emails or pictures will download (i.e., would appear on your computer from the Internet). However, this will also depend to some degree upon the quality of your phone line. Many phone lines have a limit to how much information can pass along them. Although sometimes there is only a slight reduction in the capability of the line in transmitting information, it can go as low as 33.6Kbps. If this is the case, your modem will be able to transmit information only at this speed, even if it is capable of delivering more. You can check the speed of your connection at *http://promos.mcafee.com/speedometer/* or *http://bandwidthplace.com/speedtest/*. It does not matter what type of device you are using to connect to the Internet – you simply click to run a test and a few seconds or minutes later you will get the results.

To log on to the Internet using a modem you will also need to set up an account with an Internet Service Provider (ISP, see below). Your ISP will provide you with a telephone number and Internet connection software on a CDROM. Your computer will probably make a series of strange noises and dialling tones as it tries to dial the telephone number that will provide it with a link to the Internet. While you are on the Internet, callers to your home phone line will get an engaged signal. If you find that you are using the Internet a lot, it may be worth investing in a separate telephone line that can be dedicated entirely to Internet access, so leaving your normal telephone line free to receive calls, or make use of a service such as BT's Call Minder, which takes messages for you if your line is engaged.

This table summarises the advantages and disadvantages of connecting to the Internet via a normal modem.

Advantages	Disadvantages
You need access only to a telephone line.	A normal modem provides the slowest type of connection to the Internet, so downloading large or complex files, such as pictures, can be very time-consuming and costly. In some cases, it may also be completely impractical.
Built-in modems come as standard with most new machines. If not, modems are cheap to buy.	You may have to double-check that the modem disconnects at the end of an Internet session, otherwise being online can prove a costly exercise.
	Modem links can be unreliable.

Tip

The best time to get online is early morning during the weekend. If you want to use the Internet during the week, try to avoid traditional business hours (9am to 5pm) and especially the afternoon, when the USA comes online.

Broadband

You may have noticed an increasing number of advertising campaigns on TV in recent months encouraging you to upgrade your current way of accessing the Internet to broadband. So, what exactly is broadband?

Usually, when you talk to someone on the phone, only a small part of the capacity of the telephone cable or line is used to transmit your voice. The rest remains unused. However, recent developments have meant that the capacity can be split to carry high-speed digital information. Broadband simply refers to technologies that make use of more of the capacity.

The term used by the telecoms industry to refer to technology that sends digital data down an ordinary copper telephone line is Digital Subscriber Line (DSL). BT and NTL are currently promoting a version of DSL which is known as Asymmetric Digital Subscriber Line or ADSL. The asymmetric bit simply means that there is a difference in the speed at which information is downloaded or uploaded (copied from your computer to the Internet). Information downloads happen very quickly, while uploading is much slower. However, most of the time you will not notice this limitation.

Using broadband means that you can be on the Internet and make or receive telephone calls at the same time. More importantly, information is transferred much more quickly. At the very least, you can expect the speed of transmission to be three times faster than a normal modem dial-up connection; it will more than likely be around ten times faster. However, the maximum speed specified is rarely achieved in practice.

The beauty of broadband is that although you will still need to pay for your telephone line and any voice calls you make (see below for the fee) you will have permanent, unlimited access to the Internet at no extra cost. And it is likely that you will be able to keep your existing telephone number along with many of the telephone services that you currently receive.

What do you need to do to get broadband?

The short answer to this is 'the right address'. Broadband is currently available only at some exchanges. If you live in a large city, broadband will be available, either from BT or from your cable TV provider. If you live in a smaller city or town, it is becoming available, but you may still have to wait a year or two in some locations. If you live in a rural area, broadband almost certainly will not be available.

But all is not lost. BT has promised to install broadband in any part of the country that shows enough interest. Small towns and even smaller village communities have created campaigns to demonstrate that enough people will use the service to make it worth installing. BT maintains a website that lists the exchanges that need to do this (see *www.bt.co.uk/openworld/*). If your exchange is on this list you can check this site to see how many more people need to sign up for BT to make the needed changes. If you feel strongly about broadband, you can try to organise a local campaign with fliers, meetings and whatever else you feel may help. To register your interest, you need to make a formal request to your current ISP, which will pass this information on to BT. In some areas, notably parts of Cornwall, BT is cooperating with local businesses which are helping to pay for modifying each exchange.

If you want to subscribe to a broadband service you will generally need to purchase an installation pack (currently in the region of £80), pay a monthly subscription charge (in the region of £25 to £30 per month depending upon the provider) and possibly a one-off connection fee. The cost of a broadband connection has come down in recent months, and some companies are waiving the connection fee and reducing the cost of the equipment. There are some very good deals to be had, so it will pay to shop around.

Some broadband providers offer different download speeds for different prices. For example, Pipex (*www.pipex.com*) offers a lower-cost download speed of 512Kbps, which can give a home user a speed that is up to ten times faster than a modem. Business users, on the other hand, with a larger number of PCs to connect to the Internet, are provided with download speeds of 2Mbps at a higher price.

Should you upgrade?
The answer depends on how much you use the Internet and what you tend to use if for. If, for instance, you:

- download lots of documents containing graphics, video or sound
- get frustrated with the amount of time you have to wait to get online
- find that web pages with graphics take a long time to load
- wish that your emails would come in a little faster
- spend a long time waiting for pages to download as you try to do your shopping or banking online
- play games or videos online

then broadband may be just the solution that you are looking for. The speed of your Internet connection and transmission of information can have a huge impact on the quality of the files that you receive. Animated pictures, videos, voice messages and music should all be of higher quality than you would receive via a dial-up connection. If you are considering communicating with someone via a web camera video link (see Chapter 6), listening to Internet radio or playing online games, having a broadband connection can make all the difference between having an enjoyable experience or having one which is intensely frustrating.

This table summarises the advantages and disadvantages of having a broadband connection to the Internet.

Advantages	Disadvantages
Speed of downloading files can be ten times faster than a dial-up modem connection.	There is a monthly connection fee, although this seems to be coming down.
You will have the ability to download complex files.	You may need to upgrade your hardware.
You will have a permanent connection to the Internet.	If you live more than 5km from an exchange or if you live in a rural area, the service may not be available to you.
Your computer will be better suited to the new generation of Internet technologies.	You may have to change your ISP as not all are currently able to support broadband connections, and you may need firewall protection.

Over 40 million households in Europe are expected to have a broadband connection by 2006.

Hardware requirements for broadband

If you are thinking about getting broadband it is recommended that you have a PC with the following specification or higher:

- Pentium II (or equivalent) 233 or above
- 32Mb RAM (although 64Mb is preferable)
- USB port
- CDROM drive
- 40 Mb hard-disk space
- Windows 98/2000/XP/ME.

Cable broadband

If you have access to cable phone or TV you may be able to subscribe to a cable broadband connection to the Internet. Two of the main contenders in this area are NTL (*www.ntl.co.uk*) and Telewest (*www.telewest.co.uk*; its broadband service is called Blueyonder). To check whether you are in an area served by cable broadband, check *www.askntl.com* or *www.blueyonder.co.uk*.

At the time of writing, NTL provided the following:

Connection speed	Installation fee/monthly charge
128Kbps (twice as fast as a standard modem)	£25/£14.99
600Kbps speed	Free/£24.99
Supremely fast 1Mb connection (20 times faster than a standard modem)	Free/£34.99

Telewest's Blueyonder broadband service (ten times faster than a modem) costs around £25 per month if you subscribe to its cable telephone service. Otherwise the monthly charge is £29.99.

Some companies providing cable and ADSL broadband allow you to link additional computers to the modem for a fee. This is something worth checking out if several members of your family regularly use the Internet.

The same benefits apply to cable broadband as with ADSL: the Internet connection is permanently on and your phone line is free to take ordinary calls. Unfortunately, the same restrictions also apply – at the moment, these services are mainly available only in larger towns and cities. If you do decide to go with cable broadband, check that your computer has an Ethernet adapter (most do). You can do this by checking the specification of your PC to see if it has a network card listed or by looking on the back of the machine for an RJ45 connector, which looks a bit like a phone socket.

Satellite and wireless

If you live in the countryside and find it difficult to get broadband access, you may be able to send and receive information directly via a two-way satellite dish (similar in a way to getting satellite TV). While you should be able to achieve a 400Kbps download transmission speed, the cost of installing and running such a system will generally be higher than with ADSL, and there may be delays which make it problematic for anyone who wants to play games online. Transmission may also be affected by adverse weather conditions. BT's satellite system is now available over the entire UK. See *www.btopenworld.com/satellite*. Note that businesses may qualify for funding help. (Details are available on the website.)

Before you go to the expense of a satellite system, ask around your local area and see if anyone else has had one installed. See if you can get a demonstration of its capabilities. If you are keen to go ahead, check the response time for technical or system support. If you live in a remote part of the country, it may be quite some time before an engineer will come out to adjust your dish should it need doing.

There are also various radio-based broadband schemes available. These are particularly popular in London and the Home Counties. Any good Internet magazine will have a list of the most current companies that can offer this service.

Accessing the Internet without a PC

Not all Internet access has to be through a PC. There are many other ways to get online and access some, if not all, Internet services.

Through a TV set

A number of companies provide Internet access through a TV set, a top box and a telephone line, and these services are proving to be increasingly popular in Europe. In fact, it is estimated that by 2008, European households will spend in excess of £1.1 billion on interactive digital TV services. Among other things, these technologies allow you to surf the Net and watch TV at the same time, participate in online surveys and access enhanced programme content such as background information on how a particular programme was made.

Freeserve has developed a version of its website (*www.freeserve.com*) specifically for a TV audience. It contains the same tools that you would find if you were accessing the site through a PC. In between watching TV programmes, you can read and send emails, order a pizza or buy CDs online – all without leaving your sofa or picking up the phone. If you want more information on this service, visit *www.freeserve.com/internettv/*. There is no subscription fee or joining fee for the Freeserve service, and online calls are charged at local rates.

An electrical retailer should be able to give you advice on the range of TV Internet services available, but before you sign up, make sure you know just how much you will be charged while you are online. Some packages include an unlimited Internet access rate while others will charge by the minute.

Wireless devices

Although the majority of people still use a PC to access the Internet, exciting developments taking place in the area of wireless technology will revolutionise the way we access the Internet while on the move. If you have a wireless device – a pager, a personal digital assistant (PDA) or mobile phone – you may already have access to a range of Internet services.

As far back as 1997 the WAP Forum was set up by Motorola, Ericsson, Nokia and Unwired Planet (currently Phone.com) to determine common standards and applications for bringing Internet content to digital cellular phones and other wireless devices. These standards became known as Wireless Application Protocol or WAP for short. The industry faced a lot of challenges at the time: hand-held devices had small screens, limited memory and could hold their power only for a short period of time. There were also limitations in the speed at which information could be transmitted across the networks. As a result, WAP phones are designed to browse a cut-down version of the Internet and are ideal for receiving small parcels of information, such as news bulletins, stocks and shares prices, sports results and email while you are on the move.

The take up of WAP phones has been something of a disappointment. People complain that there are too few WAP Internet sites (although the number of sites is increasing) and that the connection to the Internet is unreliable. Things look set to change, though. Technologies that allow data download speeds comparable to accessing the Internet through a dial-up modem have recently been introduced, as have new location-based services. It is now possible for your WAP phone to pick up your location and tell you where the nearest petrol station or restaurant is.

Most mobile phones currently use a Global System for Mobile technology (GSM) that connects to the Internet at 9.6Kbps. (At around one-sixth of the speed of a dial-up connection, this is very slow indeed.) Recent technological advances, such as the General Packet Radio Service (GPRS) and Universal Mobile Telecommunications Systems (UMTS), promise to change the face of mobile Internet access. GPRS provides a much speedier and permanent connection to the Internet (up to 115Kbps) and UMTS (the next generation in mobile phone technology) will enable you to receive video and audio. With GPRS, you pay for the volume of information downloaded, not for the time you spend connected. However, GPRS is still far more expensive than a home connection, and there is no equivalent of the fixed-price payment schemes available to home Internet users.

Mobile phone users can now do many things that were previously impractical. You can:

- send multi-media messages (text, sound and pictures)
- use WAP services
- send and receive email (including attachments)
- chat with friends
- link your mobile to a laptop or hand-held PC and surf the Net.

GPRS also brings with it the potential for doing online transactions, such as banking and shopping, while on the move. You can also use it in conjunction with remote access software so that you can tap into resources that are stored on your company network.

To use these Internet facilities you will need a mobile phone that is configured for GPRS. Check out some of the websites of the major phone companies and look for options relating to Internet access. Pay particular attention to each operator's tariffs, which vary

---

Internet kiosks

At the time of writing, BT has installed over 1,200 multi-purpose Internet kiosks countrywide, with a plan to increase the number to 20,000 by 2008. The kiosks have colour touch-sensitive screens that you can press to navigate your way through lots of interesting Internet sites. You can browse up-to-the-minute news, sports and weather, and get maps and information on shops and eating places in the area.

The kiosks give you the option to make ordinary telephone calls but you can also choose to send text messages to mobile phones and send and receive emails. The majority of kiosks will have a high-speed broadband connection to the Internet.

At the present time, most of these blue telephone boxes or *e-payphones* are located in major high streets, but BT intends to expand the service and place them in airports, shopping centres, and train, bus and tube stations.

---

hugely in value and usually include a minimum fee you will have to pay whether or not you use the service.

Other interesting developments include various smartphones. These combine the power of a small PC with a phone. Getting the balance between weight, size and ease of use right is a perennial problem, but for those who want an address and phone book, a notepad, calculator and perhaps also access to the Net and a full email service, they offer more facilities than a typical small phone without the weight and bulk of a full-sized laptop. New models are appearing all the time. For the latest developments see *Which?* or *Computing Which?* magazines.

Internet Service Providers

Although you may have the necessary equipment to connect to the Internet you will still need access to the many networks that make up the Internet. Companies that provide you with this access are called Internet Service Providers (ISPs). Broadly speaking, ISPs invest in and manage extensive computer networks and provide links to other networks across the world so that you can send and receive the information you want. ISPs vary in the services that they provide and what they charge for them. An ISP will provide you with a physical connection to the Internet and software that helps you to make the most of its services.

ISP services offer a range of options, including:

- access to the World Wide Web
- one or more email addresses
- access to newsgroups (Usenet)
- space so you can post your own web page.

Things to consider when choosing an ISP

Speed, reliability and performance
Speed is a key issue for most people. If the aim is to use the Internet to make your life easier, a slow and unreliable connection can be very off-putting.

If you see yourself surfing the Net regularly, purchasing items online or sending/receiving emails with photographs or voice messages attached, you should look for an ISP which will provide you with a consistently fast and reliable connection to the Internet. Many ISPs publish information as to how reliable they are. You should typically expect to be able to connect to the Internet first time on more than 90 per cent of occasions. You might excuse a slight dip in this during peak times, but not by much.

Ask friends who have an ISP:

- do you usually get connected to the Internet straight away or do you have to wait a while because the line is busy?
- once connected, do you manage to stay connected or do you sometimes lose the connection during an Internet session? If the latter is the case, how often does this happen?
- do you have to wait a long time for web pages to download?

Help

If you are a relatively inexperienced user of the Internet, check whether your ISP is able to provide you with support if you get stuck. Things to check include the following:

- is there a helpline?
- will there be a separate charge for this service or is it covered as part of your package? Some ISPs charge up to £1 per minute for calls to their helpline
- will you get to speak to a real person or will you have to rely on some other means of communicating, such as via email (which could be impossible if your Internet connection is down)?
- will help be available around the clock or only at specific times of the day/evening/weekend? Consider whether this will be convenient for you
- how long will it be before you can expect a response from a query?
- does the ISP publish a set of Frequently Asked Questions (FAQs) and/or up-to-date information about its service?

Multiple email addresses

Some ISPs allow you to have several email addresses. This may be particularly useful for families who want to receive mail separately.

Creating a website

If you are considering setting up your own website, look for an ISP that will allow you space to store your web pages. The amount of allocated storage space differs between ISPs. If all you want to do is put in a little text and some pictures, 10Mb will probably be enough. If you want to use large multimedia files, look for an ISP that will give you around 50Mb of space.

Cost

Last, but not least, check out the general charges. Some ISPs, such as Freeserve, are free to join and charge you only for the calls that you make. Each time you connect to the Internet it will cost you the price of a local call. Others, such as Which? Online, AOL (America OnLine) and CompuServe, charge a monthly connection fee on top of call charges, but justify this by providing content and additional benefits for members only.

You may be wondering why you would want to pay for ISP services when you can get them free. The answer, as always, depends upon what you are looking for. You may find that you can get the speed, performance, reliability and support you require only by paying a monthly subscription fee. Other reasons why you may choose one ISP over another is that it can host your website or because you like the information and services it provides through the members section of its website. On the other hand, you may be satisfied that your needs can be met through a free service provider. The best advice is to do your homework and shop around.

Before you subscribe to an ISP check out some Internet magazines and look for reviews or comparisons of their performance and services. Most, like *Internet Magazine*, do this on a regular basis. Visit a range of ISP websites and compare what is on offer. For a list of free, unmetered and broadband service providers, visit *www.net4nowt.com*.

As a rule of thumb, if you use the Internet for fewer than ten off-peak hours per week (evenings and weekends), consider a *pay as you go* tariff, so that you pay only for the time that you are connected. If, on the other hand, you use the Internet a lot, you can make savings by subscribing to a package which enables you to dial up to the Internet an unlimited number of times for a set monthly fee.

Services

ISPs such as AOL and the Microsoft Network are a special case. They offer their own private network of users and a collection of magazine-like features that change regularly, as well as access to the rest of the Internet. These services are a good choice for more casual and less technical users because they need the bare minimum of skill to use. They also make it easier to socialise. More experienced users may find them a little frustrating, as the facilities they offer remain basic and are very hard to customise.

Tip

The Internet Services Providers Association provides a list of ISPs which have made a commitment to follow good business practice and abide by a set code of conduct. You can find its website at *www.ispa.org.uk.*

Chapter 2

Searching the World Wide Web

Learning to navigate your way around the World Wide Web can be difficult but it will prove to be rewarding. This chapter first explains what browsers are and then shows you how to find the information you want efficiently and easily.

Web browsers

Web browsers are software programs that allow you to view web pages in all their graphical glory. A web page is written in a language commonly understood by computers around the world but not by the average visitor to the web. HyperText Markup Language (HTML) is one such language. Among other things it specifies what should appear on the page and how it should be presented. For example, a page might contain HTML codes that position the main heading at the top right-hand side of the screen and in large, bold, colourful text. Your web browser will interpret the codes for you and all you will see is the end result. If you would like to see HTML for yourself, click on 'View source' in the browser window the next time you are logged on to the Internet.

Usually your Internet Service Provider (ISP) will provide you with browser software as part of your subscription package. Although Internet Explorer and Netscape Navigator remain the most popular browsers, there are other contenders in the field. Opera, for instance, aims to provide the best Internet experience for all users irrespective of the device they are using, and gives particular consideration to the difficulties experienced by the physically impaired. It also claims to be the fastest and least memory-intensive browser around; judging by the number of awards it has collected, these claims seem to be substantiated. You can download Opera for a 20-day trial period, after which you can purchase the full version for around £25. For more information visit *www.opera.com/*. Other browsers include Mozilla (*www.mozilla.org*) and Safari (*www.apple.com/safari*).

As the web evolves and information is presented in an increasingly sophisticated manner, it is a good idea to keep your browser software as up-to-date as possible. Visit your browser website regularly to see if there has been a recent release of the software and if your PC can work with the latest version (the site should advise you of this), look for an option to download.

Although instructions contained in this chapter refer to Internet Explorer, similar tools and options can be found in other browsers.

Using your browser

To open up your browser either double-click the icon representing it on your desktop or click the Windows Start icon, choose 'Programs' and then the name of your browser.

Your browser will load a window from which you can now surf the Internet.

Finding what you want

Websites and web addresses

A website is made of one or more related web pages. Each website has its own unique address, which is similar in a way to having a unique house address and is your link to finding what you want on the web. A website address is officially known as a Uniform Resource Locator or URL.

An address is made up of a collection of different characters. The first part of the address (the 'http://' bit) means that the site is written according to a set of web standards called Hypertext Transfer Protocol. These allow you to view the page on the web. Following http:// most addresses contain the letters 'www' to represent the World Wide Web.

The final part of the address is usually a word, such as a company name, followed by a full stop and a few letters that signify the type of organisation (also known as a domain), as below.

Extension	Type of organisation
.com	Commercial (often associated with American companies)
.co.uk	UK company
.net	Associated with international companies
.org	Generally associated with organisations that are non-profit making
.ac	Academic institutions
.gov	Government institutions

An address may also have an extension to associate it with a particular country. Here are some examples.

Extension	Country	Example site
au	Australia	National Library of Australia at *www.nla.gov.au*
in	India	A one-stop shop for all Indian government websites at *www.goidirectory.nic.in*
is	Iceland	The Icelandic Tourist Board at *www.icetourist.is*
it	Italy	Italian airline Alitalia at *www.alitalia.it*
sg	Singapore	The National University of Singapore at *www.nus.edu.sg*

If you know the address of a website that you want to visit, you can open the first page of the site (known as the 'home page') by typing the address straight into the address line of your browser screen.

Tip

When you are typing an address into your browser address line make sure that you type upper and lower case letters in appropriate places and include all other characters such as hyphens and full stops. You don't need to enter the http:// part of the address as your browser will automatically enter this for you.

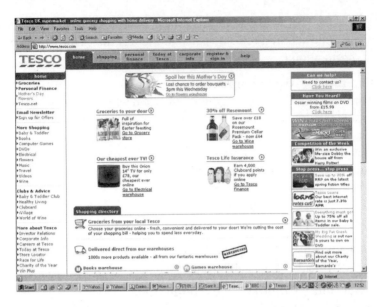

The address in the screen (*www.tesco.com*) above will take you to the main page for Tesco's online store. Tesco's website is a collection of lots of web pages each relating to different departments throughout the store. On the screen below is the web page for the video warehouse. It has a different address from the home page. The address for this page is *www.tesco.com/entertainment/vision.htm*.

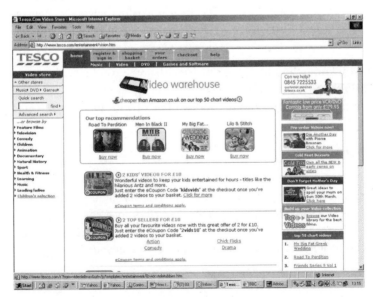

Hyperlinks to other pages

A major attraction of the Internet is that you can move easily and quickly from one page of information to another. On most web pages you will find words which are underlined and sometimes displayed in a different colour to the rest of the text. If you put your mouse over these words and the pointer shape changes to a hand, you have found a *hyperlink* – an address of another web page that is embedded in the current page. If you click on a hyperlink you will go to the address of the new page. For example, if you go to an online shopping page such as the one for Tesco shown at the top on the facing page, you will see lots of hyperlinks to different 'departments' around the store.

Links to other pages are not always in the form of words. Sometimes the link (also known as a *hotlink*) is embedded in a photo, a picture, a button or an icon. In all cases, a link will take you quickly and effortlessly to related information. Moving from one page or site to another is known as *surfing the Net*.

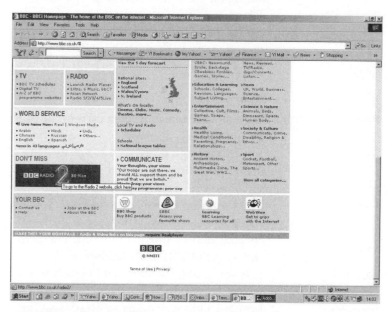

The BBC site featured above has a link to the Radio 2 website, as well as to a list of BBC products, favourite TV shows, learning resources and tips on how to use the Internet.

The Internet Explorer Screen

Whatever you are looking for on the Net, it will help you to become familiar with your browser. At the top of the browser screen you will see:

- a title bar that shows you the name of the website you are visiting
- a set of menu choices
- an address bar that you can use to type in the name of the next website to visit
- a toolbar containing buttons that will help you to navigate the Net.

Some useful toolbar buttons	Description
Back	Takes you to the last page that you looked at during the current session on the Internet
Forward	Takes you forward through pages you have visited. This is activated only once you have clicked the Back button
Stop	Stops a loading page in its tracks. It is especially useful if the page seems to be taking a long time to load
Refresh	Refreshes the screen if some parts of the page are not properly displayed. It is also useful if you are visiting a page (such as a chatroom) that is regularly updated and it is some time since you last looked at it
Home	Takes you to your pre-set home page. You can change this, when your browser is open, by clicking 'Tools', 'Internet Options' and then changing the URL in the address line
Search	Lets you search for information when you type in keywords
Favorites	Lets you add a web page to a list of favourites or access a page that is in your current favourites list

History	Shows you a list of web pages that you have visited recently. Press Control H for a shortcut to the history list
Mail	Allows you to send or receive email
Print	Prints the current web page

Favorites

A favorite (or a bookmark) is a way of marking an interesting site so that you can come back to it at a future date, much like you would use a bookmark to turn quickly to a page in a paper book. Before you create a favorite, decide which page of the site you want to return to and move to it. Ask yourself whether you are interested in a specific page (don't forget that website content changes frequently), or whether it would be best to return to the site's home page and find your way from there?

To create a favorite, click the 'Favorites' button on the toolbar, then 'Add'. You then have a choice of simply adding it to a list (click on 'OK') or creating a folder – organised perhaps by subject – in which you store the link (click on 'Create in an existing folder').

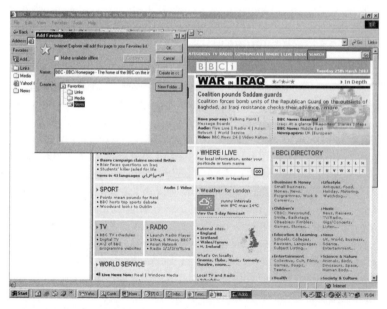

In this example, the BBC home page is being added to a folder called News.

To load a web page that you have previously bookmarked, click on the 'Favorites' icon, select the folder it is stored in and click on the file containing the bookmark.

Searching the Net

A search engine is a software program that has been specifically designed to help you trawl through the vast amount of information available on the Internet. This is no mean feat as there are literally billions of pages of information and no standard way of categorising them all.

Finding what you want on the Net can sometimes be a time-consuming and frustrating process. However, you can greatly improve your chance of success by enlisting the help of a dedicated search engine and employing a few special searching techniques.

Search tools

To find information on the World Wide Web you could use the 'Search' button on your browser's toolbar, but it would be more effective to use a search engine, a subject directory or a metacrawler.

How do search engines work?

Search engines use software known as robots or spiders to trawl the World Wide Web and collect information from as many websites as possible. They typically index words on publicly available pages of a site and deposit their findings in a huge holding file known as a database. Because they scan through each page word for word, they are particularly useful when you want to find sites that contain key-words, phrases or other unique word combinations.

When you use a search engine to search for keywords you are in fact searching the database of the search engine and not the entire World Wide Web. The result will be a list of sites that contain your keywords, ranked in order of relevance as determined by the search engine (different engines use different methods for ranking sites). Although spiders and robots regularly revisit sites to search for and update information that has changed since their last visit, when you carry out a search you are actually searching a static database of information that may have been captured a little while ago and not be a live up-to-the-minute part of the Net.

Using search engines undoubtedly brings some frustrations but they are still the best way you have of finding information on the Net. To go straight to each search engine, type its web address into the address bar of your web browser. Google (*www.google.co.uk*) is an example of an effective and well-respected search engine. Type in keywords that describe what you are looking for and click on 'Google search'. The search engine will then scan its database and retrieve links to any web pages or related items containing those words. Some search engines will also let you search for images.

If you know exactly what you are looking for, such as information on the James Bond film *Dr No*, you can use a search engine to search for those key-words. However, because of the way in which search engines index words, only a few of the sites listed may be relevant to your particular search.

Web pages are being constantly updated and new sites appear as quickly as others disappear, so information can change. As each search engine has its own particular way of sifting through the infor-mation out there and keeping up to date with new information, it means that no two search engines will come up with the same results. In fact, it is estimated that only 60 per cent of information is common across search engines and the rest is unique to the particular engine that you are using. So, if you can't find what you are looking for, try an alternative search engine. Also, try using a few of the more popular search engines to search for the same information and compare the results. That way, you will get a feel for those that you prefer.

The most popular search engines, apart from Google, are:

www.yahoo.com
www.hotbot.co.uk
www.lycos.co.uk
www.altavista.com
www.northernlight.com
www.ask.co.uk
www.about.com

Subject directories

Subject directories are categories or directories of information that are thought to be of interest to the general public. Whereas search engines use automated programs to collect information, subject directories are compiled by real people. An editorial decision is made as to what kinds of information the general public is likely to be interested in. Subject directories are a useful way of browsing general topics of interest such as education or health.

Some of the more popular subject directories are listed below. These directories provide lists of websites under subject headings compiled by human editors.

www.yahoo.com
www.google.com
www.altavista.com
http://dmoz.org
www.looksmart.co.uk

The Open Directory at *http://dmoz.org* claims to be the 'largest, most comprehensive human-edited directory of the Web' and is maintained by volunteer editors. If you are interested in making a contribution to this global community project all you have to do is visit the site, look for a subject that you know something about and sign up as an editor.

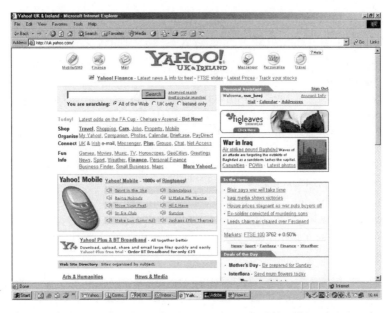

Yahoo! provides categories and sub-categories of information related to the keywords that you have entered. When you make your final choice from a sub-category you are offered links to sites related to your chosen topic.

An increasing number of specialist subject directories are popping up. These are directories that list websites that may appeal to specific target groups or contain links to specific interest sites. For example, there are search directories aimed at specific age groups like *www.yahooligans.com* compiled by Yahoo! or *http://sunsite.berkeley. edu/KidsClick!/* compiled by librarians, both for children, and *www.50connect.co.uk/* for the over 50s.

Whether you use a search engine tool or go for a directory listing depends to some extent on the style that you feel happy with and the type of information that you are searching for. These days, the distinction between the two types of search tool can be a little vague as some search engines also provide subject directories and some subject directories use search engines to search their directory database or link in to other resources on the web.

Metacrawlers

Rather than relying on the results from individual search engines, metacrawlers or meta-search engines will search multiple search engines at the same time and list the top best matches found by each. Once you have submitted a search it is transmitted simultaneously to the databases of several search engines. Some metacrawlers merge the results from each of the search engines into a single list while others display the results from individual search engines as separate lists. Metacrawlers do not have their own web page databases.

MetaCrawler, found at *www.metacrawler.com*, searches top search engines such as About (*www.about.com*), Google (*www.google.com*), Yahoo! (*www.yahoo.com*), AltaVista (*www.altavista.com*) and Ask Jeeves (*www.ask.co.uk*).

Other meta-search engines can be found at the following addresses:

www.dogpile.com

www.gogettem.com

http://vivisimo.com

Although meta-search engines are particularly useful when you want to carry out a quick and simple search, they retrieve only the top 10–50 results from each search engine, and so the total number of hits may be fewer than by doing a direct search using an individual search engine. Also, few search Google, one of the top search engines around.

Getting the most from your search engine

Sometimes it can be difficult to find the exact information that you need from a search engine. But there are lots of things that you can do to achieve more meaningful results. One of the first steps is to think carefully about the keywords that you will use as the basis of your search. Try to find keywords that best describe what you are looking for. Make use of unique keywords, combinations of keywords, synonyms and phrases. You will find that a little forethought can pay real dividends.

Many search engines will also give you tips on how to get the most from your search using their particular software. Look for and read the help pages on the search engine website that will give you advice and tips on searching. Look for a button, hyperlink or similar which will give you options for advanced searching and be aware that techniques do vary from search engine to search engine.

The first rule of thumb is to be selective in the words that you use. For instance, let's say that you want to find information on mental health nursing practices in Australia. If you simply type **nursing** as your keyword, you will get a list of sites that cover general areas related to nursing and not those specifically related to mental health nursing in Australia. Far better to use the words **mental health nursing Australia** than just **nursing** on its own. However, the opposite can also be true. If you type keywords that produce a fruitless search, it may be that the words you have used are too specific or unusual. Try to think of alternative words to describe what you are looking for. For example, **mental health nursing** might also be referred to as **psychiatric nursing** on some websites.

Boolean logic

Most search engines support the use of characters or words (used in logical operations) to refine a search. Check the help pages of the search tool you are using to make sure that it supports the use of the following commonly used search characters listed below and give them a try.

Search characters	What they do
+	Most search engines allow you to use a plus symbol before a word to specify that the word must be displayed in the results. For example, a search string such as **+Perth +Australia** would only find those sites where both the words **Perth** and **Australia** are mentioned.
-	On the contrary, preceding a word with a minus symbol would indicate that you do not want sites containing the word to appear in the results. This can be very helpful in narrowing the focus, especially if you have to wade through lots of sites that are on the fringes of the topic that you are really interested in. So, **+Perth +Australia –Scotland** would look for sites that mention Perth, Australia but not Scotland.
AND	Similarly try using the word **AND** to find documents containing all of the specified words or phrases. **Nursing AND Australia** will generally find documents containing both the word nursing and the word Australia.
OR	If the word **OR** is used to separate words in the search string, the search engine will look for documents that contain at least one of the specified words or phrases. For example, **nursing OR Australia** will find documents that contain either the word nursing *or* the word Australia but not necessarily both.
NEAR	The word **NEAR** can be used to find documents where specified words and phrases are within 10 words of each other. **Nursing NEAR Australia** will bring up documents that mention both nursing and Australia in the same sentence or paragraph.

"Quotation marks" When you type several keywords into a search box (e.g. **+psychiatric +nursing +Australia**), the search engine will look for pages that contain all three words. However, the fact that the words appear in the same document doesn't necessarily mean that the document will contain the information you are after.

The word **psychiatric** within a document might refer to a list of psychiatric hospitals and the word **nursing** might appear in an article on the shortage of nursing staff in a particular region. To make sure that the search will bring up documents that contain the words in the particular context you are interested in, place quotation marks around the phrase.

The search engine will look for an exact phrase match and will show you only links to pages where all the words appear together in the exact order specified. For example **"psychiatric nursing homes in Brisbane"** will only show you links where these words appear together on a page.

★ An asterisk (known as a wildcard) can be used to allow partial matching. For example, typing **math★**; will find math, maths, mathematics, mathematician and so on.

In general, the more information you type in each field, the shorter and more accurate your results will be.

Tip

If you want to check out several links listed in a search engine's results, right click each link that you are interested in and choose 'Open in new window'. Each website will then open in a window of its own. This is useful because you don't have to keep using the 'Back' button to get back to your search results again and also because sometimes you may want to view the contents of more than one of the results page at the same time.

Cookies

You may be surprised to know that finding what you want on the Net can be a two-way relationship. You don't always have to search for things that you are interested in – sometimes things come to you! A good number of websites are keen to know who you are, what you like, what you are interested in and what other websites you have visited. When you enter personal details or make choices, many sites store this information on your computer in a text file called a *cookie*. A cookie can be read only by the computer that created it. The idea is that when you visit that site again, the cookie will help the website to recognise you and fine-tune the content so that it is of interest or use to you. For example, it may be that while you are shopping online a cookie will be created that enables the website to remember what you put into your shopping trolley, even if you log out of the site.

The majority of cookies are used to good purpose. They may hold information about your login details, which will save you time when you come to load the website again. They may also remember your preferences for particular products or services or register your interest in particular pages. Of course, there will always be some unscrupulous sites out there who make use of this information to advertise products or services to you that you don't want.

Controlling cookies

So, what can you do to control cookies? The answer is quite a lot. It would be unrealistic to suggest that you should never give personal details out because lots of sites request that you fill in registration details before you are allowed to access their services. If you want to receive a newsletter, for example, you will need to give your email address. However, you should give personal details only if you feel that the site is secure and reputable and even then you can limit what you contribute by completing only those fields that are mandatory and leaving all others blank.

Where possible, review the privacy policy of the site that you are visiting and find out what it does with your information. Many, like *www.microsoft.com*, have a strict privacy code and although they build a personal profile of you, in theory you should be able to see and amend it at any time. In practice, though, it may prove difficult to track down all the individual pieces of information that make up your profile. So, if you are in any doubt, don't give it out!

Your web browser will also provide you with additional control over whether to accept cookies on your machine and from whom. If you are using Internet Explorer, select the 'Tools' menu followed by 'Internet Options' and click on the 'Privacy' tab. Security settings go from high to low on a sliding scale. The default setting is medium. Move the slider to the bottom if you are happy to accept all cookies or to the top if you want to block all cookies and prevent existing cookies being read. Bear in mind, however, that some websites rely on depositing cookies on your hard disk and may not be able to load properly if you have restricted their access.

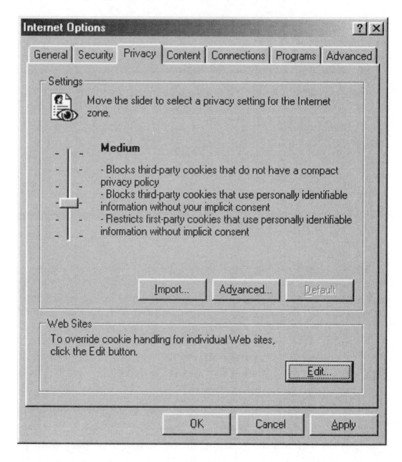

If you set your privacy to high, medium high, medium or low, you can click the 'Edit' button in the 'Internet Options' dialog box and enter the names of websites that should never be allowed to save cookies to your machine or, conversely, those that should always be allowed. If you want to override automatic cookie handling, click the 'Advanced' tab and choose your settings.

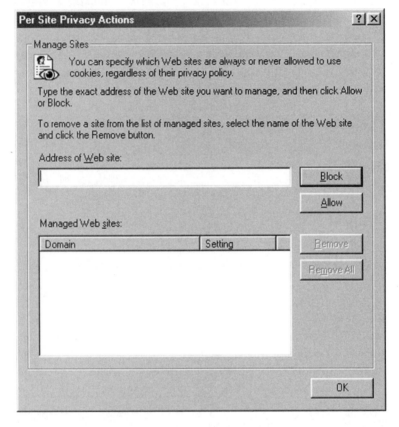

Windows stores cookies in a folder called Temporary Internet Files. If you want to see these files from within Internet Explorer, select 'Tools', 'Internet Options' and click the 'General' tab. Click the 'Settings' button and then 'View files'. The folder stores web pages and other files, such as cookies and graphics, as you view them. This store is also known as a *cache*. You can work your way through the list and delete those files that you no longer want or you can move back to the 'General' page of 'Internet options' and choose to delete all cookies or temporary Internet files from your hard disk to free up space. If you are using Netscape Navigator, you will need to look for a file called Cookie.txt on your hard disk (or MagicCookie in the 'Preferences' folder if you are using a Macintosh).

Chapter 3

Children and the Internet

Computers and the Internet are now a part of children's everyday life, and while the Internet is undoubtedly of great use to young people, it also has a darker side. This chapter starts by looking at the vital issue of children's safety on the Net, and then goes on to suggest sites that are of special interest to children.

Keeping children safe on the Internet

The first step in ensuring that children are safe on the Internet is to understand the threats posed by the Net. There are two main sources of danger to children: they could come across unsuitable sites while surfing the Net, and/or they could 'meet' undesirable characters through email contact or in chatrooms.

Despite high-profile reports in the newspapers about the dangers of the Net, one in two children report that their parents never supervise them online, according to a report in 2002 by the Cyberspace Research Unit at the University of Central Lancashire. A further one in ten reported that they had attended a face-to-face meeting with another chat user and, worryingly, three out of every four who went were not accompanied by an adult.

Research carried out by BMRB for BT Openworld in October 2002 seems to corroborate this: it found that 41 per cent of parents with children between the ages of nine and 16 do not supervise their child online, either by sitting with them or by using filtering tools.

These are shocking statistics but they do not mean that you should ban your child from going online. Education, parental supervision and technology can all ensure that your child's experience on the Internet continues to be informative, fun and safe.

Two important common-sense tips on how to achieve this are:

- keep the PC in the main living area, so you can keep an eye on what your children are doing. This can become a problem with older children, especially those who want to play loud games (don't forget that earphones can be used instead of speakers), or want the privacy to gossip electronically with their friends. There is no perfect solution here, and the line between intrusive surveillance and privacy is something parents will have to decide for themselves

- with older pre-teens and teens talk honestly about the dangers and set ground rules. Accept that if your child visits a friend's home, he or she may have access to the Internet without any restrictions. That is why education is a good policy.

Technical solutions also exist to help keep your child safe online. However, it should be stressed that short of looking over a child's shoulder every minute that he or she spends online, no solution is 100 per cent foolproof. A number of technical steps you can take to enhance your child's safety on the Net are discussed in depth below.

Searches on the Net

A search on the Net can easily throw up unsavoury material. Additionally, mistyping an address can result in a nasty surprise. Some websites deliberately mimic the addresses of well-known children's sites to attract them to their site.

Other sites may use 'meta tags' to attract more hits. Meta tags are keywords that are included within the header of the home page of a site. Search engines use them or keywords to find sites (see Chapter 2 for more on searching). If your child is searching using a keyword, he or she could quite innocently come across an objectionable site that has used that same keyword as a meta tag even though it bears no relevance to the site's content.

Search engines for children

Search engines are simply special websites designed to allow you to search the World Wide Web for specific information. They are free to use and there is a wide selection to choose from (see Chapter 2). Some search engines limit their searches to sites

47

considered appropriate for children or ones specifically designed for children. By restricting the options such engines can make it easier for children to use the Internet. The only drawback is that occasionally they can prevent them from accessing valuable information on other sites. Child-friendly search engines can also provide some protection from inappropriate material, but they are not an alternative to using filtering software (see *Internet filters*) as children can easily stray to other areas of the Net.

Typing a casual search term into a search engine such as Yahoo!, say, usually produces thousands of results, not all of which relate to the original enquiry. For example, a search for sites which reference 'Lord of the Rings' returned 2,090,000 web-based matches using the standard Yahoo! search engine. Not all of these would have been suitable for children. Fortunately, Yahoo! (among others) produces a child-friendly version of its search engine, called Yahooligans! (*www.yahooligans.com*). This search engine is specifically aimed at 7–12-year-olds, and has search topics categorised into directories relevant to the target age group. This child-friendly search engine only returns a list of websites that have not been blocked by its team of editors, which is employed to manually check and filter out any inappropriate or objectionable sites from a list of 'good sites'. Yahooligans! is pretty effective, according to a survey by *Which?* (June 2000), which concluded that the search engine did not return any offensive sites. However, Yahooligans! tends to be restrictive – an identical search on 'Lord of the Rings' produced just 31 results.

Other child-friendly search engines such as Altavista Family Filter block sites based on inappropriate material. Rather than working from a restricted list of acceptable sites, the search facility starts with a full list and filters out those sites containing unacceptable words and phrases as well as objectionable images and audio or video clips. In addition, some pages are also flagged for removal by the site editors as well as other Altavista users. In general, this type of search engine is designed to filter out sites considered unsuitable or inappropriate, such as those that deal with explicit sexual topics, pornography, violence or hate speech, drug use and gambling. Altavista does provide a degree of parental control by offering the facility to filter only audio, images and video (the default), filter all web pages or turn the filtering off.

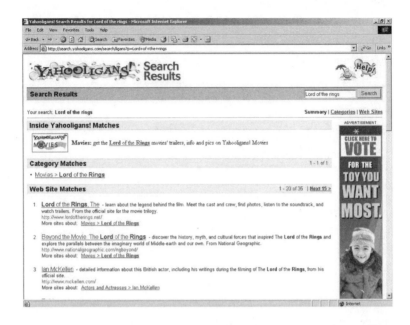

The *Which?* survey found this type of search engine less efficient at blocking unsuitable sites than 'good list' search engines, such as Yahooligans!. On one search, 45 of the sites Altavista returned were considered unsuitable for children owing to their sexually explicit nature. When accessing the full directory of the Altavista search engine (*www.altavista.com*), a search for 'Lord of the Rings' resulted in 58,777 web-based matches. When the 'For Kids' directory was selected, the search returned 1,169 matches and the 'For Teenagers' directory returned 2,144 matches, in both cases considerably more than the Yahooligans! filter.

Ask Jeeves for Kids (*www.ajkids.com*) has a completely different approach to searching. Based on the popular adult version – where you ask a question and Jeeves, the butler, attempts to find the answer – children are encouraged to use full-sentence questions rather than keywords. Jeeves will attempt to provide an answer to the question using sites that have been selected by an editor. The sites included are chosen based on quality, depth of content as well as safety, with many being written specifically for children. This stringent level of filtering provides no scope for parental control, which can prove frustrating for older children. When searching for 'Lord of the Rings', Ask Jeeves for Kids provided a choice of two routes: to find out more about *The Lord of the Rings* or find out more about Tolkein. Both options provided text containing links to other relevant information.

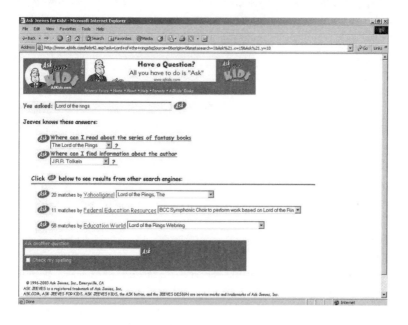

Tip

Your choice of search engine depends on your priority. If you are willing to risk the possibility of some undesirable sites slipping through, go for an engine that filters based on keywords and phrases, such as Altavista. Your children will then have a greater choice of sites and, consequently, access to more information. If you want to be more confident that your children will not be exposed to unacceptable sites, go for one of the search engines that hand-picks appropriate sites such as Yahooligans! or Ask Jeeves for Kids. But remember, children can easily stray to other areas of the Internet and you will also need to ensure that your computer is installed with filtering software (see *Internet filters*).

Case history

Mike has three children aged 5, 7 and 10. They all use the Internet – the youngest less frequently than the other two. Being aware of how easy it is to come across unsuitable websites, Mike decided to install a child-friendly search engine for when the children were searching for homework-related information. On the recommendation of a friend he plumped for KidsClick! (*www.kidsclick.org*). Backed by librarians in the USA, KidsClick! lists about 5,000 websites in various categories.

'I went for KidsClick! because I liked the idea of the kids being able to choose from categories. KidsClick! is intended to guide users to good sites, not block them from "bad" sites. I particularly liked its selection policy. It does not catalogue sites that:

- offer only particular product/ordering information. In order to be catalogued, commercial sites must contain entertainment content or educational content
- have unsafe privacy features, i.e. sites that ask for children's full names and addresses/phone numbers
- require a fee to gain access

- celebrate evil, shock or scare, or advocate violence, hatred of other groups of people, or illegal activities
- are in obvious violation of copyright laws.

To my mind these are sensible selection criteria.'

Internet filters

The search engines discussed above provide protection only when children are searching for information. Internet filters take protection a stage further and block unsuitable material however it is accessed.

The majority of filters use a combination of methods to prevent access to objectionable material. The most common methods involve:

- using a list of **banned websites** so that your child will not be able to access a site that is on the list
- trawling for certain keywords and **banning sites** that contain them
- **blocking pages** that contain certain barred words or phrases.

In each case, it is important that parents download updated lists of sites or keywords on a regular basis, otherwise the software could become out of date. You can usually do this by accessing the product provider's website, although some providers offer a service whereby they automatically update the list for you.

Some filters take a **'walled garden'** approach. Walled gardens offer the highest form of control and protection, providing a list of approved sites and barring access to all sites not on the list. Some providers undertake all of the selection and vetting of sites, while others allow subscribers to supplement and amend the lists by typing in the addresses of additional sites or removing sites from the list. This is a good approach for quite young children, and it is (to an extent) how some child-friendly providers such as AOL (*www.aol.co.uk*) work.

To provide flexibility for families with children of varying ages, some filters use a combination method: younger children can access only those sites that are on an approved list, while older children can access all sites that are not on a banned list. If this is a requirement, make sure that the filter you choose allows you to do this. The majority of dedicated filtering software provides for multi-user settings. Cyber Patrol (*www.cyberpatrol.com*) is a good example of a family-friendly product that allows you to specify settings for every member of the family, with their own levels of filtering. Products that provide filtering as part of another feature, such as virus protection software, often provide settings for the computer as a whole and not for individual family members. Zone Alarm Pro with Web Filtering is an example of this (*www.zonelabs.com*).

Browser protection

Your existing software, notably your web browser (the software application that is used to find and display web pages), can afford some degree of protection but it is no substitute for specialist filtering software (see *Specialist filters*, below).

Microsoft's Internet Explorer, which is the most commonly used web browser, contains some built-in security options within its Content Advisor. It relies on self-rating tags (see *Website ratings*, below) when determining website content, making it far from infallible. The filtering includes only websites, not chatrooms or email, but it does provide some protection and is worth using. To access the options, go to the 'Tools' menu and select 'Internet Options'. Now click on the 'Content' tab to reveal a series of options covering language, nudity, sex and violence. This system can be password-protected to prevent children from switching the settings back.

When you first turn on Content Advisor you will find that it is set to the most conservative (least likely to offend) settings. You can change these settings for each member of your family by:

- adjusting the ratings for language, nudity, sex and violence
- adjusting the type of content other people can view with or without your permission
- setting up a list of websites that other people can never view, regardless of how the sites' contents are rated
- setting up a list of websites that other people can always view, regardless of how the sites' contents are rated
- changing the ratings systems used.

You may consider this to be adequate for your family needs, but it is worth considering some of the additional features available with specialist filtering software (see *Additional features*, below).

Protection from your ISP

Your Internet Service Provider (ISP) will usually provide a filtering service. As this filter is often available at no extra cost, it is worth finding out whether it meets your requirements. Probably the best-publicised offering is from AOL (*www.aol.co.uk*). Its product is certainly on a par with the products offered by companies providing specialist filtering software (see *Specialist filters*, below). You could also sign up to specialist children's ISPs such as Kidz.Net (*www.kidz.net*) in addition to or instead of your current ISP. These ISPs limit access to approved child-friendly sites. This can prove limiting and they are only really suitable for young children.

Specialist filters

If you are not satisfied with your ISP's offerings, you can subscribe to a number of specialist providers such as Net Nanny (*www.netnanny.com*), Cyber Patrol (*www.cyberpatrol.com*) or Cybersitter (*www.cybersitter.com*). Look at the websites of the providers and consider the additional features that may be required by your family (see *Additional features*, below) before making a decision.

Additional features

Internet filters provide a number of extra features. The list below could help you make an informed decision about the type of filtering software that is right for you and your family.

Self-rating by category: In general, it appears that filters are more concerned with barring sexually explicit materials than drug- and violence-related content. However, you can get filters that categorise sites based on content areas such as sex, drugs, violence and intolerance, and which allow you to select which categories to block. Sites that fall within these categories are given ratings, which means you can also specify the level of blocking that you want to set for each. This allows for greater parental control when specifying the types of sites that can be accessed. Clearly, the software is only as good as the controls set by the parent. The browsers Internet Explorer and Netscape work in this way, allowing you to pick the category and level of content to block. For example, when defining the levels for language, the settings range from inoffensive slang to moderate expletives through to explicit or crude language.

Tip

Before making your choice it is worth spending some time studying independent reviews of the different filtering services available. *Which?* and *Computing Which?* regularly feature articles comparing Internet filters. The individual product reviews also detail the features available with the product, so you can check that a product has all the elements you would find useful. It is certainly worth checking out the latest report before making a decision. The Parents Information Network (*www.pin.org.uk*) also offers a range of reports detailing how easy it is to install and use a range of Internet filters. It also provides details on the effectiveness of the product and security and support issues.

You can usually purchase filtering software from the providers' websites and many offer a free trial. Cyber Patrol, for instance, offers a free 14-day trial of its filtering product. You will find that the majority of products are priced comparatively. For example, at the time of writing Cyber Patrol cost £27 for a year's subscription and Net Nanny cost £24 at the current exchange rate.

As mentioned earlier, it is important to remember to keep your filtering software up to date. You will need to download a current version of the list of banned sites and words on a regular basis. You should receive instructions on how to do this when you purchase or acquire your software.

Setting a time limit: Some filters, such as McAfee's Parental Control (*http://uk.mcafee.com*), Cyber Patrol and Net Nanny allow you to restrict the time your child spends online. The filter can also set the software to allow access only at specific times of the day. This has obvious advantages if you are paying for your Internet connection based on usage. It can also be used to moderate children's use of the Internet and outsmart those children prone to night-time surfing.

Recording the site log: This feature logs the sites that your child has visited or attempted to visit. Cybersitter is just one of the filters offering this feature. However, this is somewhat intrusive. Moreover, parents should bear in mind that it is easy to stumble across sites unintentionally when one is surfing the Net, and should not chastise their children for the odd visit or attempted visit to an inappropriate site.

Modifying lists: Some filters, such as Cyber Patrol and Net Nanny, allow you to modify the list of good and bad websites. This feature provides the opportunity for you to add sites that you personally find offensive that may not be included on the bad list. Equally, if you feel that the list is too stringent you can remove sites that you are happy for your children to access. You can also add a greater range of sites to the good list. This allows for more personalised parental control.

This is a useful feature to have because some filters block innocent sites. This is usually caused by a misinterpretation of context. The barring of the Middlesex Cricket Club's site is a frequently quoted example. The banning of the word 'sex' can also prevent access to informative sex-education material that is designed for a teenage audience. Not all Internet users are happy for a third party to determine what information their children can see. In the main, the 'bad site' lists are compiled in the USA, where general censorship is more stringent than in the UK. There are also concerns that information may be blocked owing to influence from pressure groups or the software manufacturer's own political or moral stance.

Blocking personal details: If your child is likely to get carried away on shopping sites, it may also be a good idea to put a block on personal details. This feature allows you to stop names, addresses and credit-card numbers being sent over the Internet. This is also a useful safety precaution if your child is frequenting chatrooms, but bear in mind that this is not enough – paedophiles tend to ask children not for their home address but for details about their school. If this is a concern, select a product such as Cyber Patrol, which has a chatguard feature that stops children typing information such as their address.

Chatrooms, newsgroups and email: It is important to be aware that some filters concentrate on web use and do not filter chatrooms, newsgroups or emails. These are all areas where children are open to Internet abuse and need policing, so do consider the inclusion of these features when choosing your filtering software. McAfee Parental Controls has an option to restrict access to applications. This can be useful for barring entry to chatrooms. Its filtering also covers newsgroups, which is not always the case with filtering tools.

Equipped with all the facts, you can decide whether an Internet filter is relevant for your family. If you decide that it is, the next step is to make a choice from the numerous products available on the market. First, consider what features are important to you.

Feature	Required?	
	Yes	No
Blocking by bad list		
Blocking by good list		
Self-rating by category		
Setting time limits		
Recording the site log		
Modifying lists		
Blocking personal details		
Filtering chatrooms, newsgroups and email		

With this list to hand, visit the websites of a number of providers and find one that best meets your needs. If in any doubt take advantage of the free trials available before you commit yourself to purchasing one of them. Alternatively, take a look at some independent reviews of filtering software (see earlier in this section for details).

Efficiency of filters
So is an Internet filter the answer to all your concerns? Unfortunately, it is not quite that simple. Despite their claims, many filters do not block all undesirable sites. This is mainly because of the filter providers' inability to keep up with the growth in number of sites on the Internet. When tested, all the filters in the *Which?* survey allowed access to some sites containing unacceptable content.

However, on a more positive note, when informed of the findings, all the providers agreed to add the sites that met their criteria to their lists of banned sites.

Website ratings
The publishers of some websites rate themselves for content such as violence, sex, language and nudity, much in the same way as film classifications. Internet Explorer and Netscape Navigator recognise

these rating codes and allow you to pick the category and level of content to block. Some Internet filters also recognise self-rating sites and use this information when compiling lists. The Australian government has introduced compulsory ratings for Australian-based sites, but, at the moment, this scheme is voluntary in the UK. Clearly, self-rating is limited in its approach, so it is not a secure way of vetting unsuitable content.

Email and chatrooms

Email and chat are some of the most popular online activities, especially among young people. It is estimated that one in five young people in the UK use chatrooms.

Email

Unsolicited email or 'spam' is an unfortunate fact of elife. Spammers do not discriminate by age but tend to send messages to any email address that they find. These emails often contain undesirable language or images, so if your child has an email account it is worth ensuring that your filtering software also covers email.

Some ISPs (such as AOL) allow you to set up a password-protected account especially for your child. AOL also includes its own anti-spam software.

Alternatively, you may want to consider an email system designed specifically for children. A British-based ISP, TownSites (*www.townsites.co.uk*) has launched KidsCom (*www.kidscom.com*), a product that is designed to protect children from e-bullying, junk email as well as unsuitable content. It works by forwarding all unauthorised email to a separate mailbox that is managed by an adult.

With younger children, you may find it easier to access your child's email account from your own. To do this, create a new connection in your email program using your children's email details. Change both your own and your children's advanced settings so that email messages are not removed from your ISP's server for at least seven days. When you log on, all your email and your children's email will be downloaded into your email inbox.

This level of parental intervention may not be appropriate for older pre-teens and teenage children who use the PC. You will need to discuss with them the best way of using email safely and wisely. If you do have real concerns, Windows XP provides a facility to allow you to view their emails. This system requires you to create the individual accounts and passwords and therefore you will be able to log on to your child's account if you have any worries about the nature of the emails being sent or received.

Chatrooms for children

There are about 5 million children who use the Internet in the UK and over 20 per cent of those are under 14 years of age. It is estimated that some 23 per cent of children who go online use chatrooms, but in the 15–16-year-age group this increases to about 41 per cent using online chat, according to research by the Parents Information Network (*www.pin.org.uk*).

A chatroom is a collection of people sending messages to each other. The conversations happen in real time, so unlike email there is no time delay before getting a response to a message.

As already mentioned, it is widely acknowledged that some adult sexual predators use chatrooms to 'groom' young people and attempt to arrange face-to-face meetings. As a result of this, in September 2003 Microsoft took the radical step of closing tens of thousands of chatrooms run by MSN, its Internet arm. This action has been widely applauded by children's charities.

While chatrooms still exist it is important to be aware of the dangers. In addition to following the safe surfing guidelines (see box below), you can restrict your child to using moderated chatrooms. A chatroom is *moderated* if a trained adult is present whenever the chatroom is open. The *moderator* is authorised to intervene and stop the dialogue if any conversation is at all inappropriate. He or she also has the authority to ban people from the chatroom.

Safe surfing rules for children

Internet filters can help in protecting your children online only up to a point, and so industry experts stress the importance of educating your children about safe online practices. Just as you would teach your child the Green Cross Code for crossing roads, you should also outline safe surfing guidelines to them. Alarmingly, 50 per cent of chat users didn't know that they should take an adult when meeting someone from a chatroom and 20 per cent didn't

---

realise that 'people in chatrooms may not be who they say they are', according to the Cyberspace Research Unit at the University of Central Lancashire.

Research carried out by BMRB for BT Openworld in October 2002 found that 93 per cent of parents interviewed believed that schools should take responsibility for teaching Internet safety. This could be because of the fact that one in five of the parents surveyed claimed to be less Internet aware than their child.

The NetSmart rules set out by the NCH (formerly known as the National Children's Homes; *www.nchafc.org.uk*) can provide a good starting point for talking about the potential dangers with your child. There are five things that a child should never do and six things he or she should always do.

1. Never tell anyone you meet on the Internet your home address, your telephone number or your school's name, unless your parent or carer specifically gives you permission.
2. Never send anyone your picture or credit-card or bank details, without first checking with your parent or carer.
3. Never arrange to meet anyone unless your parent or carer goes with you and you meet in a public place. People you contact online are not always who they seem, even people who become penfriends or 'keypals'. People don't always tell the truth online – no one can see them.
4. Never open attachments to emails unless they come from someone you already know and trust. They could contain viruses or other programs which would destroy all the information and software on your computer.
5. Never respond to nasty or suggestive messages. Always tell your parent or carer if you get such messages or if you see rude pictures while online and report them to your Internet Service Provider.

1. Always keep your password to yourself, do not share it with anyone.
2. Always check with your parent or carer that it is okay to be in a chatroom.
3. Always be very careful in chatrooms. Even if a chatroom says it is only for children, there's no way at the moment to tell if everyone

there really is a child. It might be an adult or an older child trying to trick you.

4. Always get out of a chatroom if someone says or writes something which makes you feel uncomfortable or worried. Make sure you tell your parent or carer.

5. Always be yourself and do not pretend to be anyone or anything you are not.

6. Always stay away from sites that say they are for people over 18 only. The warnings are there to protect you. Adult sites can sometimes cost a lot more on your phone bill too.

A number of websites also outline safe surfing guidelines.

Useful websites

Chatdanger	*www.chatdanger.com*
Childnet sites	*www.childnet-int.org*
Kids Smart	*www.kidsmart.org.uk* (specifically for 8–11-year-olds)
For Kids By Kids Online	*www.fkbko.co.uk*
NetSmart rules set out by NCH	*www.nchafc.org.uk*

It is also important that your child knows that he or she can come and talk to you if someone makes inappropriate advances online or tries to arrange a face-to-face meeting.

Safety in chatrooms

The BT Openworld research found that despite the fact that more than half the parents surveyed worry about what their children are exposed to online, 45 per cent were not concerned by their children chatting to strangers on the net.

The Home Office's Internet crime forum has published *Chat Wise, Street Wise*, a report highlighting the dangers posed to young people using chatrooms. The report strongly advises children to use only chatrooms that are moderated by a known moderator. It recommends the use of rooms that have topics advertised in advance, as the BBC's do. It warns against the use of rooms with advertising or other links that can draw children away from a group environment. The report advises that parents and carers must consider the following questions before allowing children to access an Internet chatroom.

1. Is the chatroom moderated?
2. Who are the moderators?
3. Has the chatroom got a clear terms and conditions policy?
4. Does the chatroom have a clear topic/subject timetable?
5. Does the chatroom have advertising or external links?
6. Does the chatroom give young people genuine opportunities to interact and shape the chat?
7. Does the chatroom have appropriate access control and password verification? Can anyone join?
8. Does the chatroom remind users about safety issues?

Tip

Your ISP may also provide a moderated chatroom. Do not assume that this will be satisfactory. Ask to see a copy of its safety policy and find out how it vets the personnel used as moderators. Also make sure that a moderator is present throughout all chat sessions and does not service a number of different sites and visit a site only on a rota basis.

As recommended earlier, if you have Internet filtering software make sure that it also covers chatrooms, newsgroups and email. Products such as Cyber Patrol from Surf Control UK (*www.cyberpatrol.com*) include a feature that prevents children from giving out personal details online.

Checking on your children

If despite taking all the steps outlined in this chapter you still have concerns, it is important to continue probing. At the end of the day, your child's safety is of utmost importance and you may need to take more drastic measures however invasive they may seem.

If you have good reason to believe your child is being stalked online by an adult through Instant Messages or Chat, you can install a keystroke recorder program that will keep a record of any online conversations. Of course, this is a very intrusive measure and should not be considered except as a very last resort. To find examples of this software, use a search engine to look for 'Keystroke recorder'.

Tip

Do not assume that Internet Explorer's History feature will provide a reliable guide to what your children are looking at online. Many children from the early teens onwards will be familiar with the History feature and will know how to remove traces of any sites they have visited.

Internet sites for children

Clearly, the Internet can be a useful way of both entertaining and educating children.

Internet sites for fun

There are numerous sites designed for children, many of which are educational as well as fun. Some sites are updated on a regular basis, with each new version introducing more sophisticated graphics and special effects. The latest Harry Potter site is a good example of just how professional some of these sites are becoming (*www.harrypotter.warnerbros.com*).

However, sophistication comes at a price, and speed can suffer. Frustration can quickly set in when it takes minutes rather than seconds to load and refresh images on the screen. With the growing trend to install broadband (see Chapter 1) in residential properties, this will become less of a problem. But for those children accessing the Internet via a modem, the best advice is to stick to the less commercial sites.

For a good balance of fun and education try *www.nationalgeographic. com/kids/*. This site is produced by National Geographic, and topped the poll for the best children's website in an article in *Webactive* magazine in February 2003.

The younger surfer is sure to enjoy the extensive range of activities on offer from the BBC (*www.bbc.co.uk/cbeebies/*). There are games, activities, stories and competitions involving all the popular BBC characters.

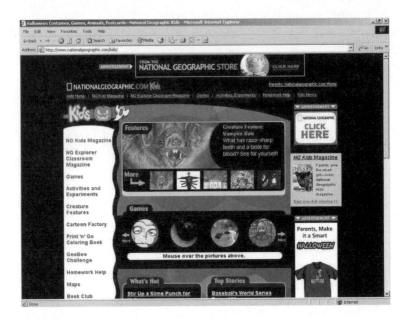

Case history

Joel, who is nine, accesses sites on the Internet on a fairly regular basis. In an average week he spends a couple of hours online.

'I usually go on the Internet at the weekend, mainly sites like Blue Peter (*www.bbc.co.uk/bluepeter*) and Mapzone (*www.mapzone. co.uk*). Mapzone is the Ordnance Survey's kids' site and it's great if you like maps! If mum has to work at the weekend I love to go with her because she's got broadband at work and it is so much quicker than at home.'

Educational sites on the Internet

Educational sites range from homework help and exam preparation to sites that teach through fun activities. Try entering 'child education' in your Internet search, and you will be presented with a huge choice. It is worth spending some time with your child to look at a number of sites and decide on a few that you are both happy with. The following suggestions may serve as a starting point, or you may want to try www.links4kids.co.uk. This directory site provides links to 18,500 sites designed specifically for children.

The under-fives

Education for the under-fives is superbly catered for by *www.underfives. co.uk*. This site provides a wealth of practical activities and includes printable worksheets for literacy, numeracy, art and craft as well as seasonal and religious festivals. If you are short on ideas for games, try the Fisher-Price site (*www.fisher-price.com/us/playtime/*). The games are categorised into those appropriate for infants, toddlers and pre-school kids.

The 5–11-age group

The child-friendly search engine Yahooligans! (*www.yahooligans. com*) nominates its top five cool sites of the week. These are often worth a look; if they don't inspire you, try looking through the past winners in the archived section. Some of the sites have an American slant but there is usually a range with worldwide interest.

The Yucky site from the Discovery channel (*www.yucky.com*) cannot fail to impress children who enjoy facts about all things yucky.

If you are looking for a specialist site, Kids Planet (*www. kidsplanet.org*) is a colourful and noisy site designed to educate on the protection of wildlife. Or, for the history buffs, try *www.schoolhistory. co.uk*. Alternatively, if you are looking for a language site, try *www.bonjour.org.uk*. This site also has links to its sister sites for German, Italian and Spanish education.

Homework sites

Homework High (*www.homeworkhigh.com*) is a Channel 4-based website with teacher-hosted live sessions. The site is designed to help students aged 16 or under. The site is 'open' from Monday to Thursday with two live sessions on each day, one in the afternoon and one in the evening, and then again on Sunday for one session in the evening. On Wednesdays there is a personal session, where trained advisers can offer those aged 11 and over general advice and help with personal questions on subjects such as bullying, stress, parents, family, friends etc. Children aged ten or less are advised to look at a Further Advice section on the personal page, or to go to an adult they can trust.

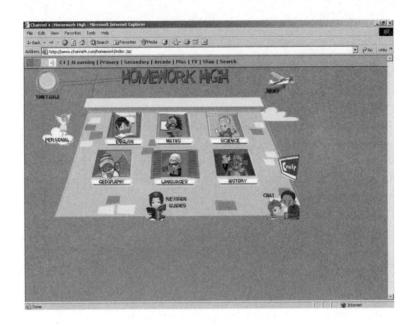

During a live session, a bank of experienced teachers or advisers waits behind the scenes, ready to help with homework problems. As soon as you send in your question, they will let you know if it is going to be answered that day. With over 200 questions being answered every day, you have a good chance of receiving a prompt reply.

Dorling Kindersley, well known and respected for its educational books for children, also has an excellent website, www.dk.com. This site provides quality information as well as clip art and fascinating facts to brighten up the dullest homework.

Exams and revision

SchoolsNet (*www.schoolsnet.com*) offers small chunks of revision for a whole range of topics, and the BBC provides a similar approach with its Bitesize Revision series (*www.bbc.co.uk/learning*).

Further education

The BT Openworld survey found that 94 per cent of the higher education students questioned use the Internet for research. Most students are experienced surfers able to track down information using an

Internet search engine. For a general information site, try the Lazy Student website (*www.lazystudent.co.uk*). This site promotes itself as the UK's most comprehensive student resource website. It provides help and advice on subjects such as education, careers and travel, and it also has a chatroom and message board facility.

Chapter 4

Family life

The Internet can prove to be of benefit throughout all the phases of family life, from planning a wedding, through the various stages of child development to the tranquillity of retirement. This chapter considers just some of the many ways in which the Internet can have a positive impact on family life.

Weddings

Weddings require planning for months if not years before the big day.

The venue

Once you have set the date, you might want to decide on a venue for both the service and reception. Checking out possible venues can prove time-consuming. By making use of the Internet, you can often reduce the options by taking a look at the venue's website. Many have interior and exterior photographs as well as details such as rates, availability and catering arrangements. Some sites also take you on a guided video tour through the venue, giving you an even better idea of whether it is the right place for your special day.

The finer details

Once you have chosen the venue, you can use the Internet to help you plan the finer details. For general information try keying the word 'wedding' and your town name in a search engine. The results will throw up sites that have national coverage, but you should also see details for more local sites. A good example of a typical wedding site is *www.confetti.co.uk*. This site provides up-to-date information on a full range of topics such as caterers, wedding shows and seating arrangements. It will also keep you up to date with current legislation regarding civil marriages. Wedding Service UK (*www.wedding-service.co.uk*) is also worth a look. This site provides one of the UK's largest online directories for wedding resources, with national as well as local links, which may prove more helpful for tracking down a photographer, booking wedding cars, ordering flowers and other local needs.

Tip

If either the bride or groom is of a different nationality or religion, you may like to take a look at *www.world-wedding-traditions.net*. This site provides information on wedding traditions and customs from around the world.

Wedding presents

The Internet can prove useful for coordinating the wedding present list. Use a site such as *www.marriagegiftlist.com*, which covers a range of stores including John Lewis, Debenhams, Marks & Spencer and Argos, or go direct to the website of your chosen store. You can browse the items on offer in the store over the Internet, and select the items you want to include on your list. Guests visit the same website to choose from your list and their selections are flagged up to avoid duplication. The presents are wrapped and delivered to you when requested. You can view your updated wedding list at any time and receive a list showing who bought what.

If you already have all the household items you need, *www. blissonline.com* is a wedding-present site with a difference. Gifts range from the bizarre to the luxurious. You can have your house cleaned, dinner parties prepared, dance lessons or be taught to become a circus clown. There are activity-based gifts and a full range of pampering treats.

After the wedding

Wedding sites also provide suggestions for the most romantic honeymoon destinations (see Chapter 9 on how to book holidays online). Another area in which the Internet comes into its own is sharing wedding photos – you can create your own website and post the photos of the wedding for all your guests to see.

Case history

June had the unenviable task of organising a wedding for her daughter in their home town in Kent, when her daughter actually lived in Australia.

'At first I thought it was an impossible task – I was dreading having to make all the decisions without Alison being here. The first hurdle was the venue for the reception. This is where I discovered the Internet.'

June found a local hotel that she thought was just right. Its website contained not only photos of the building and the grounds, but also a video providing a guided tour of the function rooms and bedrooms.

'It was great because Alison could take a look for herself and make up her own mind. After that there was no stopping me. If a supplier didn't have a website I didn't consider it. Alison picked the cake, her flowers and even the bridesmaids' dresses through Internet sites. When she returned to England a week before the wedding it was all organised!'

The Which? Guide to Getting Married gives more details on how you can use the Internet to organise your wedding.

Parenting

Numerous sites, both general and specialised, offer information and guidance on raising a family.

Babies and toddlers

Fertility, pregnancy and birth are topics covered by many sites. As with all websites, search for those belonging to reputable organisations. For general information on pregnancy and birth, try the site of the National Childbirth Trust (*www.nctpregnancyandbabycare.com*). A site called Dr Foster (*www.drfoster.co.uk*) provides comparative information on every hospital maternity unit in the UK.

Once the baby arrives, you can use Babies Online (*www. babiesonline.com*) to announce the happy occasion to the world. In just a few minutes you can create a free web page with a photograph of your baby plus a message.

Parenting websites provide practical advice on all aspects of caring for babies and toddlers. Take a look at *www.ukparents.co.uk*, *www.babyworld.co.uk*, *www.bbc.co.uk/parenting* and *www.familiesonline. co.uk*. Expect to find information on a broad range of baby- and toddler-related topics including teething, tantrums, health matters, ideas for parties and outings, suggestions for combining work with parenting, as well as products and discount offers. Many parenting sites have chatrooms or discussion forums where you can seek advice from other parents. Clearly, the answers you get will be based on experience rather than science, and you must make up your own mind whether or not to act upon it.

The Gingerbread site (*www.gingerbread.org.uk*) offers support and advice for those bringing up children alone. The site includes a chatroom, details of groups in your area and links to other related information and resources. It also offers translations into nine different languages including Welsh, Urdu and Punjabi. For the more mature mother, try *www.mothers35plus.co.uk*.

Parents whose children suffer from an illness or disability will find plenty of help and support available on the Internet. Dedicated organisations exist for a huge range of childhood problems, and many have informative and helpful websites. To track down these more specialised sites, search for the relevant term with a search engine. For more general support and problem-solving, try sites such as *www.parentlineplus.org.uk* and *www.fathersdirect.com*.

Naming your baby

Choosing a name for your baby can prove a challenge. If you are stuck for ideas, look no further than Baby Names UK (*www. namingbaby.co.uk*), which provides over 10,000 names to choose from. To find out what the most popular names are in the UK try *www.statistics.gov.uk*. This site has statistics on the top 100 boys' and girls' names for the last five years as well as practical advice on registering your baby's birth.

Buying baby products

Once the new baby arrives, finding time to go out to the shops can be hard, so the Internet can be handy. There is a huge range of websites specialising in providing shopping online for baby-related products.

To find national and local sites, search using the words 'baby products' followed by your town or county name. This will provide a listing of both national directories and regional outlets.

Alternatively, try specific sites such as *www.twoleftfeet.co.uk*, which is one of the UK's leading sites for baby goods. Featuring over 5,000 products, the site is easy to navigate and provides photographs of the products so you can see exactly what you are buying. Mothercare's site (*www.mothercare.com*) offers a familiar range of products. For a listing of smaller, independent retailers try *www.ukchildrensdirectory.com*. If you are on the look-out for a bargain, *www.discountbabystore.co.uk* claims that all of the goods listed are up to 50 per cent cheaper than the retailer's recommended price.

For more information take a look at *The Which? Guide to Baby Products*, which also includes plenty of advice on shopping online.

Case history

John and Cathy live in Essex and are expecting twins. Although delighted at the thought of a double addition to the family they were less happy at the prospect of having to buy another set of baby products. They had assumed that their two-year-old daughter's cot, high-chair and pushchair would service the new baby and there would be little need for extra expense. Fortunately, a friend told them about a site called Webswappers (*www.webswappers.com*) that specialises in second-hand items.

'The site was really easy to use. We selected the 'Parenting and babies' section and then chose the 'Prams/pushchairs' category. Luckily for us there were four pushchairs on offer in Essex. Because Essex is a big place we needed to email the owners of the one we particularly liked the look of to find out where they lived. They weren't too far away so we drove over at the weekend and got ourselves a bargain!

'One thing that did put us off though was the registering, because we thought we would have to pay. But we soon realised that the service is free, so it wasn't a problem. I think we were also fortunate that there were a few pushchairs to choose from. We weren't so lucky with a cot. There were only two on offer, both in the north of England. When the twins are older we will certainly try to sell our baby equipment through a site like this.'

Another popular site for buying nearly-new goods is eBay (*www.ebay.co.uk*), a shopping auction site. With this site you find an item that you are interested in and place a bid. If your bid proves to be the highest you get to buy the item. For more details on how auction sites work, see Chapter 7.

What not to buy second hand

Steer clear of buying second-hand mattresses or children's car seats. The former could be soiled and harbouring germs, and the latter could easily have internal defects without showing any visible signs of damage.

Pre-school childcare

Finding someone you can trust to look after your child can be both stressful and time-consuming. There is no easy answer but the Internet can provide some choices. Start your search by entering the word 'childcare' along with your town or region in the search box. The list will include national organisations as well as local childcare providers. One site that includes a range of options is *www.childcare-online.com*. This site provides links to sites offering the services of professional nannies, mothers' helps, au pairs and babysitters. Some of the linked sites provide personal details of people in your area currently seeking positions with families.

In addition to services matching parents with childcare professionals, some sites also provide advice and general information on employing someone to help with childcare. It is worth taking the time to read this.

The Daycare Trust (*www.daycaretrust.org.uk*) is a national childcare charity committed to promoting high-quality affordable childcare. The website is designed to help parents find out more about childcare so that they can make the right decisions for their children.

For further information and links to relevant sites in your locality try *www.childcarelink.gov.uk*. The Government launched the ChildcareLink website in December 1999 as part of the National Childcare Strategy. This strategy aims to help people back into the workplace by providing information about the different types of childcare and early education available locally. Including information from over 170 local authorities, ChildcareLink is supported by the Sure Start Unit, the Scottish Executive and the Welsh Assembly as part of their National Childcare Strategies.

Schools and education

The Qualifications and Curriculum Authority (QCA) publishes a recommended scheme of work that supports the National Curriculum for England and Wales. It outlines the range of topics that your child should cover in each year of his or her school education. If this is of interest to you, take a look at *www.qca.org.uk*. The site provides information on all areas of the curriculum for both primary and secondary education. The Scottish guidelines for education are documented at the Scottish Qualifications Authority site (*www.sqa.org.uk*).

Information on Northern Ireland guidelines can be found at *www.qca.org.uk/ni*. Alternatively, try the Northern Ireland Council for the Curriculum Examinations and Assessment (*www.ccea.org.uk*).

Choosing the right school

What you need when choosing a school for your children is reliable information. The reputation a school has may bear little resemblance to its true academic performance. The Internet can prove a useful tool when carrying out your own investigations.

The government provides a site detailing performance tables for primary and secondary schools and post-16 establishments (*www.dfes.gov.uk/performancetables/*). This site also details national pupil absence information. It is easy to use and is designed to provide information on a named school or by postcode. To find out about schools in a particular area of the country, simply type in a postcode and the radius – in terms of the number of miles – from the postcode that you want to search. From the list that appears you can then select individual schools for detailed information. This is an extremely useful facility if you are moving to a new area of the country.

Some newspapers, such as *The Guardian*, also provide an interactive guide for schools (*http://education.guardian.co.uk*). You will find options to view the league tables for both primary and secondary schools. There are three sets of figures for each local education authority (LEA): general school statistics; GCSE/GNVQ performance figures; and A-level/AGNVQ performance figures.

Helping your child study

Children are introduced to information and communication technology (ICT) at school during the nursery or reception years. The official curriculum for ICT starts in year 1, when your child is five or six years of age. He or she will also be encouraged to use computers and the Internet when working within other areas of the curriculum and for projects and homework. For children, the Internet is just another tool in the learning process.

Internet search engines are invaluable in helping research topics for projects and homework. Children can search on subjects ranging from the Vikings to space probes. In many cases the problem will be information overload rather than not enough results. But if your child is using a child-friendly search engine (see Chapter 3)

Educating parents about the Internet

The Parents Information Network (*www.pin.org.uk*) is an independent service helping parents to support their children's learning through the use of computer software and the Internet. Established in 1994, PIN provides a wide range of advice on educational and safety issues for parents. This site provides up-to-date, independent evaluations of both software and websites. It is worth taking a look at it before buying new programs or introducing your children to Internet sites. *Which?* also regularly features reviews of new software and sites. You can either track down back issues at your local library or access them on Which? Online (*www.which.net*), which is a subscription-only service.

The Department of Education and Skills (*www.parentsonline. gov.uk*) also provides a website specifically designed to help parents understand the educational benefits of the Internet, including suggestions on how parents can become involved in their children's online learning.

and cannot find enough information, it is advisable to supervise him or her using an adult version of the search engine.

Most websites have a print option so your child can print out relevant pages and work away from the computer to compile his or her own version of events. Most teachers have grown wise to children handing in printed pages from the Internet and can also spot meticulously copied accounts!

Helping children with their school work can be a taxing experience. After all, it was probably years ago that you learned about the invasion of the Vikings and it's doubtful that you have given it much consideration since! If you need to brush up your own knowledge so that you can help your children, try *www.topmarks.co.uk*. This is a directory site providing a parents' section as well as links to sites that can help you with a full range of subjects from art to sociology. Alternatively, try *www.learningalive.co.uk* for online resources for parents, teachers and children. Curriculum experts select all the articles and there are links to over 4,000 other relevant sites.

For further information on using the Internet for homework and revision, see Chapter 3.

Understanding SATs

If you are interested in seeing what a Standard Assessment Test (SAT) paper looks like, take a look at *www.gridclub.com*. This site has a section called SATs Magic, which provides an option to download sample SATs papers for Key Stages 1 and 2. For more general information on the British education system, try *www.educate.org.uk*, a site designed for teachers but also of interest to parents.

Education initiatives and policy

For current initiatives and reviews try the BBC's schools site, *http://www.bbc.co.uk/schools/*. This popular site includes a section designed specifically for parents, providing access to current, topical articles as well and previously published articles. The parents' page also provides access to a downloadable newsletter called *Together* and news items concerning educational issues.

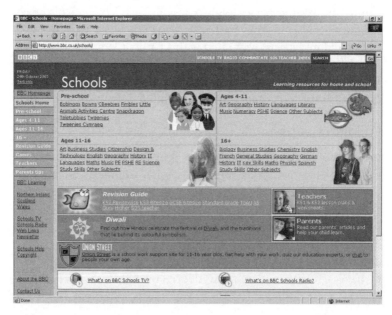

The Department for Education and Skills (DfES) also provides online information for parents (*www.dfes.gov.uk/parentsgateway*). This site provides details of government policies as well as advice on practical topics including childcare provision, bullying initiatives, grants and qualifications.

Advice on bullying

For specific advice on bullying try *www.antibullying.net*. The Scottish Executive has established this site to enable teachers, parents and young people to share ideas about how bullying should be tackled. The site provides excellent advice on self-help for children as well as useful tips for parents on how to navigate the school and legal guidelines to make sure the bullying stops. Although aimed at children, the Childline site, *www.childline.co.uk*, also includes some useful information for parents.

Celebrations and parties

Family life is interspersed with occasions to celebrate – birthdays, religious events and anniversaries to name but a few. They all call to be marked in a special way, often with a party or family get-together. The Internet can prove invaluable when organising such an event. Whether you simply need help or you want someone to take it all out of your hands, you can usually find a solution by using the Internet.

Children's parties

If you are looking for a site to provide all the answers, try *www.kids-party.com*. This site has it all – venues, entertainers, theme parks, cinema listings, fancy dress hire, party merchandise and much more. If you want to hand it all over to someone else you can also find a local party organiser to sort it out for you. If you do decide on a DIY party, remember that the art to hosting a great children's party is keeping them busy and it is always a good idea to have a few games up your sleeve. Eventwise (*www.eventwise. co.uk*) is a site designed for organising a corporate event, but it also has an excellent section on party games. Select the 'Party animals' option from the menu. Partyzone (*www.partyzone.co.uk*) is another useful site providing plenty of advice and tips on how to host the perfect children's party. There are suggestions for planning the party, ideas for suitable parties for children of different ages and lots of party games to keep the children entertained. The site's shopping area provides everything you need for a hassle-free party: food boxes, paper cups and plates, party hats, birthday cakes and the all-important party bag.

Religious and cultural occasions

To keep abreast of religious festivals from around the world, take a look at *www.multicultural-matters.com*, which provides a list of all the festivals that fall within the current month. If you are particularly interested in the culinary side of festivals try *www.holidayrecipe.com*. This site seems to have a recipe for every religious, cultural or national celebration going.

If you are looking for more specific information try searching for the name of the country or religion followed by the words 'festival' or 'celebration'. This should provide a list of possible sites.

Special family occasions

Wedding anniversaries, birthdays and family celebrations often call for a special meal. Whether at home or at a restaurant the Internet can help you organise the event.

Eating out
On a special occasion you want to make sure that everyone can relax and feel comfortable, and getting the venue right is paramount to the success of the event. If you are going to have children in the party, for example, check that the restaurant is happy to cater for them.

Your best bet is personal recommendation. Failing that, you could use the Internet to search for restaurants in your area which advertise that they cater for family parties. Try using a search engine to search for 'family-friendly restaurants'. Include the name of the town or area to restrict the search. Alternatively, try *www.yell.co.uk*, the online version of *Yellow Pages*. This should provide ample choice and will often give links to the websites of individual restaurants.

Dinner party

If you decide on a family dinner party at home, the Internet can help. By searching on the word 'recipe', you will uncover thousands of sites. Many independent wine merchants and supermarkets offer online purchasing of wines and spirits. For example, see *www.oddbins.com*. Wine Pages (*www.wine-pages.com*) offers comprehensive information on wine, including food and wine matching.

Presents

If you are finding it difficult to come up with a present with a difference, try *www.activitysuperstore.com*. This site has hundreds of ideas, ranging from bungee jumping and white-water rafting through to family portraits, adopting animals and loads of pampering treats. Presents Direct (*www.presentsdirect.com*) is another site worth a visit. It has a gift-finder option that allows you to specify a category for the recipient, such as baby, teenager, man, woman and even pet. You can also enter a minimum and maximum price for the gift. The search will come up with a number of ideas, all of which can be purchased online.

Buying presents for children can be an exhausting task, especially around Christmas time. Alleviate some of the stress by shopping online. Many of the high street stores provide an online shopping service: try *www.elc.co.uk* for Early Learning Centre toys and *www.mulberrybush.co.uk* for an interesting range of traditional toys and games.

Family outings and holidays

Finding something interesting to do during school holidays, on a wet weekend or while on a holiday in an unfamiliar part of the country can be trying. Fortunately, there are numerous sites designed to help you out. To find a list of local offerings, enter the words 'family day out' in a search engine, followed by the town or region. You will access some local sites as well as a full range of directory-type sites that provide countrywide information. The national sites typically offer a way of specifying the region of the country as well as the type of activity you are interested in. The choice can range from activity camps through to zoos and safaris.

A good example of this type of directory can be found in *www.daysout.co.uk*.

Select the 'Search all' option and choose to search by region, attraction name or a distance from your postcode. The Allkids site *www.allkids.co.uk* provides a similar service. Select the 'Days out' option from the parenting information box. This site supplements its offering by having links to websites providing up-to-date information about the weather, road maps and traffic news – all important factors when arranging a day out.

Wherever you are in the country the National Trust (*www.nationaltrust.org.uk*) is sure to have an attraction close by. Its site is attractive and informative, providing details on over 612,000 acres of countryside and more than 300 historic buildings and gardens that you can visit.

Getting away for a child-friendly break in the UK is simple with *www.childfriendly.co.uk*. This site is billed as a child-friendly travel and restaurant guide. Select the area of the country that you are interested in and then filter your search based on the type of accommodation required, such as hotels, B&B, self-catering or caravans. If you are a member of Which? Online, you could access *The*

Case history

Ali and Ria found themselves on a caravan site in Cornwall during the wettest week of the summer. With two children aged seven and nine they knew that they had to find somewhere to go for at least part of the day.

'Luckily we had stumbled across an Internet café in a local town so over a cup of coffee we managed to track down a couple of sites listing family days out. One was a national site with quite a few options in our area. The other was a local information site. It was brilliant: it had details on swimming pools, cinemas and an ice-skating rink. They were all listed under *Things to do on a wet day*. They must be used to rain in Cornwall!'

Which? Guide to Good Hotels and *The Good Bed and Breakfast Guide* and again search for child-friendly establishments. For holidays with a difference, try the British Activity Holidays Association (*www.baha.org.uk*) and select 'Holiday search'. You are presented with a number of options including family activity holidays. The list of venues is not extensive but it will provide a starting point.

For more options try *www.ukchildrensdirectory.com*. Type 'holidays' in the search box for a list of related sites. If you want general information on travelling with children take a look at *www.travellingwithchildren.co.uk*. This site provides a wealth of information from packing tips to health and safety. It also has a shopping section from which you can buy travel essentials such as children's sunglasses, travel beds and car safety accessories.

For further ideas on how the Internet can help plan your holiday, see Chapter 9.

Retirement

When you have retired you may have time to indulge in some of your interests. It may be that you have always wanted to try painting, or you fancy learning a new language. Whatever your aspirations, the Internet can prove an excellent starting point.

A number of sites cater for the over-50s. Sites such as *www.seniority.co.uk* act as a directory providing links to other sites that may be of specific interest to 'silver surfers'. A site called 50Connect (*www.50connect.co.uk*) is a portal aimed at the over-50s providing news, reviews, chatrooms and links to sites specifically catering for the more mature Internet user. This site is a good place to start if you are new to the Internet.

If you have a specific interest, try using a search engine to search for a keyword relating to that subject. If the resulting list is too extensive, restrict the search by including further keywords. For example, searching on the word 'painting' will produce a range of sites from art galleries through to painting and decorating services. Try being more specific and enter a search string such as 'painting classes Nottingham', and you may strike lucky.

Case history

When Cliff retired he went out and bought himself a top-of-the-range computer with a printer, scanner and large screen. Over the last ten years he has had his money's worth, so he has recently invested in a replacement model. On the whole he has used the computer for two main hobbies: photography and genealogy. Cliff says, 'Over the years

families have become more and more disparate, often with branches as far flung as Australia and the USA. The Internet is the perfect tool for research.

'I started my research by looking at the census information *www.census.pro.gov.uk*. It took me a while to find my way around but it was worth persevering. My next find was the Rootsweb site *www.rootsweb.com*.

This site has proved extremely useful, subscribing is free and it produces a monthly newsletter that is full of interesting articles. Family Search (*www.familysearch.org*) is another good site. It is run by The Church of Jesus Christ of Latter Day Saints and provides a lot of information from unusual sources. Genealogy is a hobby I would recommend to anyone. Over the years I have received and given help to fellow researchers from Cornwall, Australia and New Zealand.'

If you are considering taking up genealogy as a hobby, try *www.genealogylinks.net*, which is a directory site that provides over 14,000 links to sources of related information.

Organising a funeral

With many people living far away from their parents, being able to organise a funeral from another area of the country or even the world can prove a necessity. UK Funerals Online (*www.uk-funerals.co.uk*) is an excellent site to help you through these difficult times. The site provides clear, factual and unemotional advice on what to do initially following a death, through to advice on legal issues, help organisations and dealing with bereavement. This directory site will also point you in the right direction for sites providing funeral services and related needs such as florists.

Chapter 5

Email

Email is by far the most popular Internet application: the number of emails sent has risen from 5 billion per day in 1999 to an estimated 14.9 billion in 2002, according to research company International Data Corporation. It is predicted that this figure could go up to 35 billion by 2005.

The basics of email

Email stands for electronic mail, a service that allows you to send and receive messages from one computer to another.

The advantages and disadvantages of email

Apart from the convenience of not having to go to a post office, email is cheaper and quicker too. You could send a message to a friend in another country and it could reach him or her within a few minutes, for the cost of a local phone call. Using email is also convenient in that you can get in touch with people without bothering them in real time – if, say, you need to contact someone who is busy during the day, you could send a message which the person can read when he or she is free. Moreover, you can attach digital photographs, pictures, video and voice recordings to your email.

It is difficult to focus on the downside of something that has so many advantages, but of course there are some things that you should be wary of. Emails tend to be more informal in tone than a letter and an email rattled off at speed is open to misinterpretation.

To avoid confusion you can use emoticons (email symbols, which denote emotions), such as a smiley ☺ to lighten the tone or diffuse an awkward situation. A winking face can let the recipient know you are only joking, while a flower shows that you care. You can create these using symbols such as the colon and bracket symbols on a standard keyboard, though some email programs do include their own symbols.

It is also easy to send an email to the wrong address. Email programs have buttons to Reply, Reply to all and Forward messages and if you hit the wrong button you could forward a personal message to the wrong person. Twenty-eight per cent of those surveyed by Yahoo! said that they live in fear of personal emails being sent to their boss by mistake, while 61 per cent of workers were afraid of a friend forwarding personal emails to their friends.

Email viruses and junk email are other serious problems, and these are dealt with towards the end of the chapter along with tips on how to keep them at bay.

What's in a name?

Before you can send and receive email you need an email address, similar in a way to having a postal address for your home. You can usually get an email address from your Internet Service Provider (ISP). It will typically contain your name or some part of it, followed by an @ symbol, the mail server's domain name and a few letters which indicate the kind of mail server being used. The mail server domain name is simply the name of the computer on the Internet that will store and forward your mail.

For example, if May Lomax's email address is Maylom@talk21. com, the opening part of the address (Maylom) is made up of her first name and the first few letters of her surname, talk21 is the mail server's domain name and .com indicates that it is the mail server of a commercial company.

When you send email from your PC it will travel down your telephone line to your ISP's server, which will then post your mail along a route to its destination, wherever that happens to be in the world. It will also receive and store email that has been sent to you, until you are ready to read it or transfer it from the ISP server to your PC.

Sometimes you will see letters signifying the country of origin at the end of the address, for example, uk for United Kingdom, au for Australia, nz for New Zealand and so on. For example, an email address for Catherine Simpson who lives in New Zealand might read *cats@xtra.co.nz*.

Tip

There is nothing to stop you signing up for additional email addresses with different providers. In fact, having several email addresses can come in handy. You could use one as your main address, and keep the others for use if you experience technical difficulties with the first provider.

Case history

Tom has two grandchildren who have recently emigrated to Australia. Both children use email confidently and have persuaded Tom to invest in a PC so that they can write and send photos to each other regularly.

'Although I was absolutely determined to get to grips with it all, I just didn't know where to begin. I felt really confused about the whole thing. I spoke to a friend who said that the first thing I needed to do was to sign up with an Internet Service Provider. I went to the website of my telephone provider to see if I could get an email address from it.

'In the search box I typed 'How do I get an email address?' One of the choices that came up was how to get a free email account. I clicked on that and registered for the free account.

'I filled in some registration details like my name and address and then I was offered a choice of email names. I thought I'd try and choose my own name instead of picking one from the list, but a message came up saying that someone else was already using the name I'd chosen. I tried another name of my choice and this time it went through okay. I couldn't believe it could be so easy.'

Using an email program

Once you have a registered email address the next step is to choose an email program or mailer that will direct mail to and from your ISP server. Dedicated email programs accompany the two main web browsers, Internet Explorer and Netscape Navigator. Internet Explorer comes with Outlook Express and Netscape Navigator comes with Messenger. You don't have to stick with the email program that is attached to your browser though; there are many other email programs out there. Generally all you have to do is to download a program from a website. Eudora is an independent, free email program (*www.eudora.com*).

Your email program will need to talk to your ISP mail server so that it can look for your mail and copy it to your PC. When you first sign up with an ISP you should be given the necessary information on how to do this. You will need to follow a set of on-screen prompts and enter some technical information.

Email on the move

One very convenient aspect of email is that you can access it when you are on the move. Some ISPs allow you to log on to the Internet from any PC in the world that has a connection and pick up your emails from their website. It just means that your mail is accessed through web pages on the Internet rather than through a dedicated mail program on your PC.

Web-based email

With a web-based email account you can send and receive mail from any computer with access to the Internet. If you can't get this service through your ISP, you can sign up for free web-based email at *www.hotmail.com*, *www.yahoo.com* or *www.lycos.co.uk*.

The fact that these services are provided free of charge means that companies such as Yahoo! need to recoup the money they spend on hosting the service. They do this by collecting information from you when you register and use this information to attract companies who want to advertise their products and services to you through the site.

Even though these accounts are free, they still provide many useful email features. Most allow you to build up an online address

book, forward useful website links to your friends and attach files to
your email.

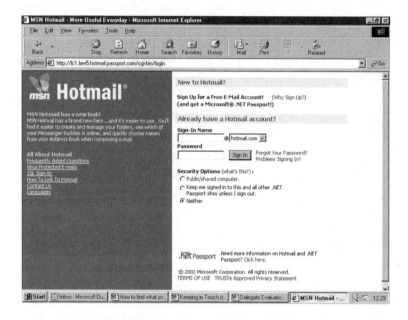

The downside of having a free account is that the ISP may allow
you only a small amount of storage space on its server for your
emails and if your files go over the size limit there is a possibility that
they will be deleted. For example, if you sign up for a free MSN
Hotmail account you will receive 2Mb of storage space for your
messages and attachments. If you go over this limit then Hotmail
may remove your messages permanently (a single large graphics file
might hit the limit by itself). To prevent this happening, make sure
you delete emails when they are finished with and, if you need to
keep them, save them locally into a folder on your hard disk.
Alternatively, you might consider signing up for a paid account. A
paid Hotmail account can provide you with 10Mb of storage space as
well as allowing you to send messages up to 3Mb in size for £19.99
per year. Yahoo! currently charges £7.99 per year for 10Mb of storage
space and £15.99 per year for 25Mb, so it is worth shopping around.

You also need to be aware that some free services will freeze your
account if you don't access it for a certain amount of time. For
example, Hotmail will freeze your account if you don't sign in at

least once in the ten days following registration and then at least once every 30 days after this period.

One big disadvantage of these free accounts is the volume of junk mail they attract. In the long term these free mail accounts may well be discontinued and you will have to pay for the service.

No PC?

You don't always need your own computer to send and receive email: you can use one at a cyber café, or use an Internet-enabled mobile phone, your TV or a telephone.

If you are going to be travelling, you will find Internet or cyber cafés in most major cities as well as in many remote parts of the world. If you visit *www.cybercafes.com* and search for the area that you are due to visit you are quite likely to find some cafés listed.

If you think you may want to access email using cyber cafés, set up a web-based email account such as Hotmail or Yahoo! before you go travelling. To set up a Hotmail account visit *www.msn.co.uk*, select the 'Hotmail' tab followed by 'New account sign up' and fill in your registration details. To set up a Yahoo! account visit the Yahoo! site at *www.yahoo.com* and select the 'Mail' tab. Follow the prompts shown in 'New to Yahoo!?'. All you need to do then is find an Internet café, type the Yahoo! or MSN website address and find the Mail tab.

Before you start using the service at a cyber café be very clear what you will be charged and make sure that there are no hidden extras. Charges can vary and may depend to some degree upon how the cyber café manages its access to the Internet. For instance, you may pay by the minute or you may be charged a flat fee per hour, plus telecoms costs. It is possible that if you try to pick up your email from an island where there are no connected links to the mainline you will be charged a high price for accessing your messages via a wireless/mobile network, so just be aware that these charges may be imposed and check them out up front.

Security is a serious issue when you are using PCs that you don't manage yourself. Be very careful about accessing bank accounts, for example, and treat any Internet café as an insecure location. The obvious advantage, however, of using such a service is that you do not have to carry around a laptop and worry about how to connect it up to local power and telecoms services.

Case history

Sue recently went on a camping trip around Europe. While in the UK she keeps in regular contact with an Australian friend and she decided to see if she could maintain the momentum by emailing from each of the places on her itinerary. She was amazed to find that all the campsites she stayed on had email facilities. The cyber café in Interlaken was the upstairs floor of a small gift shop on the site, with two computers available to use. Sue was quoted a price per minute in Swiss francs and signed a login sheet to record the time that she began her Internet session. She has a free Yahoo! account so all she had to do was visit the Yahoo! website, type her Yahoo! ID and password and pick up her email.

'It was brilliant to be able to chat away to someone the other side of the world and share my experiences, especially as my friend had also visited Interlaken in recent years. I guess the only frustrating part was keeping an eye on the clock to make sure that I didn't run up a big bill and also getting to grips with a Swiss keyboard.'

If you live near a city centre you may have noticed blue Internet telephone kiosks appearing around the main shopping areas. BT plans to install 20,000 of these countrywide over the next five years. If you have set up a web-based email account with Yahoo!, Lycos or Hotmail, you can use these kiosks to send and receive email while you are out and about. Even if you don't have your own email account you can still send email to someone who does. Just type your message, type the address of the person to whom you are writing and send. BT also provides its own web-based email service, which you can set up through *www.btbeyond.com*. There is no charge for setting up an account but calls made from a BT Internet kiosk will cost you 10p per minute, with a minimum charge of 50p.

It is also possible to configure a WAP (Wireless Access Protocol)-enabled mobile phone to dial up an email service and download your emails directly. This is usually limited to the text part of messages only, and just the first part of the message (limited by the storage capacity of the phone). The messages are displayed in the same way as text messages. This area is developing quickly and, with the newer phones able to send and receive pictures, the capabilities in mail are likely to grow rapidly. You have to set up a phone number for the email provider's mail server in your phone for the service to work. The providers tend to be specialists in this area, often working alongside your phone company and you have to pay an extra charge for the privilege.

If you don't have a WAP phone but you have a mobile phone, you can sign up for a mail alert service, such as the one provided by Yahoo!. All you need is a mobile phone with one of the main UK mobile phone companies (O_2, Orange, T-Mobile or Vodafone) and a Yahoo! email account. You will receive a text message on your mobile phone as soon as an email comes into your Yahoo! account. The message will tell you who the email is from and the subject. You can then opt to have the content of the email downloaded as a text message (or several messages if it goes over the text message limit). You can also reply via your mobile phone and Yahoo! will send your reply back as an email message. The Yahoo! mail alert service costs from as little as 11p per message, depending upon the package that you go for.

If you work away from home on a regular basis and you have a personal digital assistant (PDA) or laptop and mobile phone you might want to subscribe to an international ISP such as Net2Roam (*www.net2roam.com*), so that you can get online anywhere in the world using a local telephone number rather than expensive international dialling fees to your ISP back home. Net2Roam has access to 22,000 local numbers across 150 countries. All you have to do is to select the country that you are visiting and click the number. And you can still continue to use any existing email accounts that you have set up back home. Net2Roam claims to have saved those consumers who were dialling internationally up to 90 per cent of Internet access charges. It might also be worth checking out MaGlobe (*www.maglobe.com/*), which offers a prepaid service that allows you to connect to the Internet from any location worldwide and with a single username and password.

Digital satellite or cable TV services such as Sky Digital also offer email. Be aware, though, that even though you pay a monthly subscription fee for your TV services, you may still have to pay an additional fee to cover the time that you are sending and receiving mail via the Internet.

Case history

Michael travels the world with his work. He has two email accounts, one that he uses to pick up his business emails and a Yahoo! account that he uses to communicate with friends while he is away.

'I like to keep my business emails separate from personal emails. That way there is no danger of confidential or private information getting into the wrong hands. I originally set up a personal account with Yahoo! so that I could pop into an Internet café or use the Internet at a hotel to keep in touch with friends. More recently, though, I have invested in a Smartphone which gives me email access from my phone anytime, anywhere.'

Sending and receiving mail on your PC

It takes just three steps to send a message: write it, go online, send it. What could be easier?

This chapter has been written with Microsoft Outlook or Outlook Express in mind. However, similar options are available in most mail programs. If you are unsure how to do something, search the help facility within the program.

How to send an email

In general:

- look for a 'Mail' button
- look for 'New' (mail or message) or similar. In Hotmail and Yahoo! you have to *Compose* email
- type the address of the recipient in the 'To' box
- if you want to copy the letter to someone else who is not the main recipient, type the name in the 'Carbon copy (CC)' box. If you want to copy it to more than one person, separate each name with a semi-colon
- type a subject in the subject box
- type your letter
- click the 'Send' button or similar.

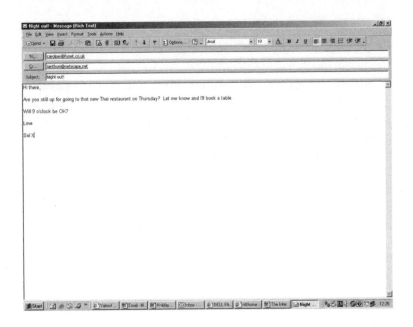

Even though you have clicked the 'Send' button your messages may not be sent immediately. They may sit in your Outbox (similar to an out tray in an office) until you click the 'Send/receive' button. If you are not already logged on to the Internet you will be prompted to connect. Once messages leave your Outbox a copy will normally appear in your Sent box. At the same time, your email program will retrieve messages that have been sent to you and they will appear in your Inbox.

Tip

To keep Internet costs to a minimum, write all your messages in one go and go online only when you are ready to send them all.

Saving a draft

If you are not ready to send a message straight away you can work on a draft version and finish it at your leisure. Simply save your message and it will sit in the Drafts folder until you open it again.

> **Tip**
>
> Text formatting is often lost unless both people are using the same 'internal' mail system. Stick to using standard Windows fonts for your text and assume that the person at the other end will get plain Courier text, with no colours, bold, italics, size changes, etc.

Open, Reply and Forward

Once a message appears in your Inbox all you have to do is double-click on it to open it. The easiest way of replying to your mail is to click on the 'Reply' button. This way, the sender's address will automatically be entered into the 'To' box and all you have to do is type your reply. Similarly, you can forward a copy of an email that you have received to someone else by clicking the 'Forward' button.

Keeping up with the housekeeping

It is a good idea to get into the habit of filing emails that you want to keep and getting rid of those that you don't.

Go through the list in your Inbox and Sent box on a regular basis. To delete messages click on a message and press the 'Delete' key on your keyboard or click the 'Delete' button in the email program. Deleted messages go into a Deleted Items folder or similar (called Trash in some programs), where they stay until you permanently delete them. If you want to reinstate a message from the deleted folder, select it and move it into one of your folders.

You can permanently remove files by selecting files in the Deleted folder one at a time and pressing 'Delete' or by choosing an option that deletes them all in one go. In Microsoft Outlook you can choose 'Empty deleted items folder' from the 'Edit' menu.

You can move or copy mail that you want to keep into named folders. Most programs provide you with standard folders such as Inbox, Outbox, Draft and Sent Items, but it is easy to make your own. To create a folder in Microsoft Outlook, select the 'New' icon followed by 'Folder'. You will be prompted to select the folder in which you want to create the new folder. Type a name for the new folder. Similar options are available in other programs.

In Outlook you can move mail into a folder by selecting the message and dragging it into the folder. In Yahoo!, you click to the left of the message to select it and then choose a folder from the 'Move to folder' drop-down list and click 'OK'.

Sorting mail

Occasionally you might find it useful to sort your email into some kind of order. For instance, you might want to quickly find mail that you have received from a particular person or look at mail that arrived on a specific date. Across the top of the screen you will see a set of column headings or tabs that tell you who sent the mail, what the subject was, the date that you received it and so on. Click a tab and your program should sort your files accordingly.

Has it arrived?

One of the most frustrating things about sending messages is not knowing whether they have arrived or not. Some programs, such as Outlook Express, go some way towards reducing this frustration by offering you the option to be notified by the recipient's system when your message has been received. If you are using Outlook Express, while you are composing a new message, click the 'Tools' menu and select the 'Request read receipt' option. Before you start composing a message you can request a receipt for *all* messages by clicking the 'Tools' menu, selecting 'Options' followed by 'Receipts' and then checking the 'Request a read receipt for all sent messages' box.

You should be aware though that the recipient can choose not to send a receipt back, and even if he or she is happy to, there are no guarantees that his or her email service will deliver the receipt back to you.

Attachments

Apart from sending and receiving messages you can attach photographs and documents to an email. To insert an attachment using Outlook or Outlook Express, click on the 'Attach' icon (a paperclip) at the top of the mail screen, browse your folders until you find the file that you want, select it and click the 'Insert' button. The attachment will appear as an icon on the screen.

There are certain factors to bear in mind, though, if you want to make sure that the attachment will arrive at its destination and that the recipient will be able to open it.

Format for success

When your recipient receives your attachment his or her computer will look to see whether it has the right type of software to read the file – if it hasn't, he or she won't be able to open it. Certain file formats are more appropriate for email than others.

If you are sending a typed document an RTF (Rich Text Format) file is preferable to a Word file because it is recognised by both PCs and Apple Macintosh machines. There are also no known viruses that can infect RTF files, whereas Word viruses are prevalent.

If you are sending a photograph a .JPG (JPEG, pronounced 'jay-peg') file is the best option as this type of picture can be opened within a standard web browser such as Internet Explorer or Netscape Navigator.

Your ISP (or the receiver's ISP) may also place restrictions on attachments because of the size or type of attachment or if it contains a virus. You will generally be notified by your ISP when a message has failed to arrive so that you can re-send it.

Tip

You can make image files smaller by saving them in JPEG format. JPEG files are compressed and take less time to send.

Viruses

A virus is a computer program that has been written with the intent of damaging the data on your PC or leaving your PC unusable. One of the main ways of picking up a virus is through opening an infected email attachment. According to a report by Sophos in February 2002, the number of known viruses in January 2002 was in excess of 70,000. Viruses spread rapidly from one system to another by infecting each program with a copy of themselves. Some activate immediately, others lie dormant until a particular trigger occurs like a specific date or time. Some viruses, such as the Stoned virus, are considered relatively harmless. It famously left a message saying, 'This computer is stoned'. Others are much more malicious.

Viruses are not the only type of program that can cause damage. A Trojan Horse is a program that masquerades as something harmless. It can appear in your email inbox as an email attachment but may be designed for more sinister purposes, such as collecting information on your passwords. More worryingly, Trojan Horses often change the 'From' line of an email address so that the email looks like it comes from someone you know. Once into your system, they can quickly spread themselves around by emailing attachments to everyone in your address book.

Picking up viruses

There are many ways in which a virus can introduce itself to your computer, in particular by:

- opening email attachments containing hidden viruses
- downloading files from the Internet
- copying a file on to your PC from an infected disk or CDROM.

Prevention is better than cure

A number of dedicated anti-virus software programs are available. Once loaded on to your PC, they sit in the background while you work, and continuously scan your files in order to detect harmful programs. Anti-virus software is constantly being updated as new viruses emerge and our ways of communicating become ever more sophisticated. As well as scanning emails, some also scan attachments in Instant Messaging programs (see Chapter 6), as well as files that you are about to download from the Internet. If they come across a virus they will either get rid of it or repair the file.

Anti-virus software is usually reasonably cheap (for example, you can buy Norton AntiVirus software from between £20 and £55) and is quite easy to install on to your PC. You typically buy a licence to use the software for a 12-month period during which time you should be eligible to receive software upgrades as they are released. As new viruses appear daily, you will definitely need to keep your software up to date.

In November 2000 the team at Which? Online tested six anti-virus products on the market. All were found to provide a high level of protection but there were variations in the level and cost of support and upgrades. Eset's Nod32, Kaspersky Lab's AVP Platinum and Symantec's Norton AntiVirus came out on top. Even if you haven't yet purchased a full-blown virus checker, your email program may afford you some protection. If you have subscribed to the web-based email service from Yahoo!, for instance, you will be offered the chance to virus check email attachments before you download them.

Things to look out for before you buy:

Features	Questions
Software enhancements	How often will you receive software enhancements and is there a cost?
Software upgrades	How often is an upgrade released and is there a charge?
Internet downloads	Can you download enhancements from the Internet?
CDROM	If you don't have access to the Internet, can you receive enhancements on CDROM and is there a charge for this service?
Email support	Can you email the software company with support queries?
Telephone support	Do they provide telephone support? If so, when is it available, for how long and at what cost?

Keeping safe

Common-sense tips to avoid viruses include:

- be wary of attachments that arrive from an unexpected source
- don't open or save attachments from people whose name you don't recognise
- make sure you download files only from a reputable source
- keep a copy of files that you really wouldn't want to lose in the event of a virus attack.

Address books

You can add email addresses and other contact details to an electronic address book and then insert these into the 'To' field of your email.

When you receive an email message using Outlook Express you can right-click the email and choose 'Add sender to address book'. Following that, all you need to do is fill in some contact details on the card displayed on your screen and save the email address into an address book. You can also add a person's email address from scratch, without ever having received email from him or her. You can do this by clicking the 'Addresses' button, selecting 'New' and then 'New contact'. As an added bonus Outlook Express gives you the option to automatically add all those people to whom you make a reply by clicking the 'Tools' menu and selecting 'Options' followed by the 'Send' tab. Choose 'Automatically put people I reply to in my Address book'.

Email is also a wonderful way of getting the same message to lots of people all in one go. If you run a group of some sort and need to contact people on a regular basis, you will find the facility to create a group folder containing the addresses of each member of the group. When you want to send email to everyone in the group, all you have to do is type the name of the group in the 'To' box. To do this in Microsoft Outlook, select 'New' from the 'File' menu followed by 'Distribution list'. Enter a name for the group and add each person's address individually or select addresses from your address book. In Outlook Express, go to your address book and choose the folder that you want to create the group in. Click 'New' on the toolbar followed by 'New group'. Create a name for the group and follow a similar procedure to add members to the group.

Autoresponse

Some email programs let you set up an autoresponse message. This is a standard message that will be emailed to anyone who sends you a message and is ideal to use while you are away on holiday or visiting friends.

Junk email

Junk email, known as spam, can be just as much of a nuisance as its paper-based relative. Spam refers to unsolicited commercial mail and includes unscrupulous activities such as promoting get-rich-quick schemes as well as mass-advertising of products and services.

How do people know my address?

Your email address can be tracked every time you visit websites and newsgroups or other areas of the Internet. There are companies which specialise in trawling the Internet collecting addresses to sell on to others.

How to minimise junk mail

Although moves are afoot to protect consumers from spam and clamp down on the culprits, it is unlikely that spam will be eradicated altogether. However, there are several things that you can do to minimise the amount of spam you receive.

Don't

- Never respond to unsolicited mail. Some will suggest that if you want to be removed from their mailing list you should reply using the word 'remove'. Don't fall for this one. If you reply it will confirm to the spammer that your email address is accurate and they will probably add you to other lists.
- Don't click on a website address contained within spam mail.
- Never give out your email address unless you know someone personally or the company is a reputable one.

Do

If you find that spamming is a serious problem, read your ISP's or email website's policy on spamming. Reputable companies generally take a very strong line against spamming (visit the Advertising Standards Authority website at *www.asa.org.uk* for more information). Most have procedures for reporting abuse and will carry out their own investigations.

In addition to the general rules above, there are other ways that you can protect yourself from spam. You can:

- use special spamming software such as the popular MailWasher program which is easy to use, free and can be downloaded from *www.mailwasher.net*. Some email programs also run anti-spamming software as standard
- filter email that comes from a particular source or contains specific words into a special folder (or the bin)
- put a block on specific email addresses.

Chapter 6

Keeping in touch

Many of the technological changes that have revolutionised communications have happened since the early 1990s. It is not so long ago that 'keeping in touch' meant sending a handwritten letter by post or having a chat on the phone. Today there are so many options for communication open to us that it can all seem a little overwhelming.

Email is the most popular of these options (see Chapter 5). But you can also attach a web camera to your PC and chat via a live video and audio link. You can use a people-search facility to track down long-lost friends or enter a chatroom and take part in real-time conversations with people you have never met.

Instant communication

Although email is an excellent way of keeping in touch with people, and is much faster than traditional 'snail' mail, it does not allow for live interaction. A number of options offer you the opportunity to do just that – communicate in real time with others.

Chatting on the Internet

Chatting via the Internet typically involves typing messages at your keyboard that other people can see almost instantaneously. There are lots of different ways in which you can engage in live discussion. You can enter an online chatroom or take part in Internet Relay Chat, either of which will allow you to thrash out ideas with large numbers of people around the world online at the same time as you. You can use Instant Messaging to have a one-to-one text conversation with an individual. Or you can engage in *real* talking by using an Internet phone. And if you want to see the person as well as talk to him or her, you can use a webcam. These options are briefly described below.

Internet Relay Chat

Before Internet Relay Chat (IRC) originated in Finland in 1988, 'chatting' on the Internet was restricted to a conversation between two people. IRC made it possible for lots of people around the world to connect to a chat server at the same time and exchange real-time text messages. Today, it is still one of the most popular ways of getting to know other Net users, with over 100,000 people chatting away online each hour of the day.

How do I get started?

To be able to participate you need to download a piece of software that will allow you to connect to a chat server. Some of the most popular programs are mIRC and Pirch for Windows and Ircle for the Macintosh. It doesn't really matter what program you use, as they all tend to connect to the same chat servers. You can install mIRC by going to *www.mirc.co.uk*. You will need to enter some details such as your name, the nickname that you want to use and your email address.

Using a nickname

Most people tend to use a nickname rather than reveal their true identity. If you are a female 'chatter' you might be wise to steer clear of names that give away your gender, otherwise you might find yourself on the receiving end of unwelcome attention.

Following the mIRC set-up procedure, pick the name of the server that you intend to use from the drop-down list or stick with the default server. All that remains after that is for you to connect to the IRC server. mIRC is a shareware product, which means that if after trying it out you are happy to continue using it, you are asked to pay a one-off fee of $20 (about £13). The mIRC website is very informative, and newcomers to this area of the Net will find it useful.

Channels

After installing mIRC you will see a list of IRC chatrooms or *channels*. The channel name represents the topic or area being explored and is preceded by a # symbol. There is no limit to the number of channels that can be created.

How do I join a conversation?

When you are ready, join a channel of your choice. If it is your first time, it would be a good idea to 'listen' to a conversation for a while until you feel comfortable joining in. Conversations can happen at a fast and furious pace and it can be very difficult at first to keep up with them, especially because any number of people can contribute to a conversation and people join and leave all the time. When you are ready to take part in the conversation, type a message on your keyboard.

Your nickname will appear on the screen along with that of the other participants, including those who are just 'listening in' to the discussion (known as *lurking*). Conversations can vary both in quality and subject matter. If you find a like-minded person and want to create your own channel, you can hide it from public view and invite that person to join you. Alternatively, if you want to enter a private conversation with someone you can usually find his or her email address from a list and carry on the conversation by email. If you are looking for intellectual debate and IRC isn't providing this for you then you may be better subscribing to Usenet or a mailing list (see sections below).

Getting started

- Explore different servers to see what channels are available.
- Before you join a channel, take time to familiarise yourself with the software by using the help and Frequently Asked Questions facility.
- Be open-minded. You are likely to meet all sorts of people online.

Chatting online in an open forum is not everyone's cup of tea. There are lots of people who will have a completely different perspective on things to you and may 'talk' in a manner that you find distasteful. Before you launch in, read as much as you can from websites that are aimed at new IRC users such as *www.newircusers.com* or *www.geocities.com/SouthBeach/Breakers/5257/Chatet.htm*. The latter site gives a humorous introduction to chat etiquette and the do's and don'ts of online discussions.

If you are the kind of person who enjoys the challenge of meeting new people, then give it a go. People take part in plenty of interesting conversations, and worthwhile information is passed around. In fact, some organisations are using this form of online conversation to get feedback from people on a number of issues. Other companies are using it as a forum for clients to ask questions and receive answers about their products. On top of that, lots of people have met their partners or made long-lasting friendships through IRC.

Web-based chatrooms
Since the early days of IRC the world of chat has moved on significantly. The most notable changes have come about through the development of the World Wide Web. Now you can log on to a chatroom (a virtual room on the Net where people meet) through a web browser without having to download special programs. Although web-based chat facilities tend to run a little slower than those provided through IRC (owing to the volume of traffic on the Net), they are usually easier to use and find your way around. You can even post images and sounds in some chatrooms.

There are thousands of chatrooms covering virtually every topic under the sun. To start with you could try checking out a couple of your favourite search engines or portals, for example *http://chat.lycos.co.uk/*.

You will also find lots of useful information at the following Yahoo! sites: *http://dir.yahoo.com/Computers_and_Internet/Internet/Chats_and_Forums/* and *http://dir.yahoo.com/Computers_and_Internet/Internet/World_Wide_Web/Chat/*.

If you are worried about coming across 'unsavoury' chatrooms, look to see what your favourite sites are offering. Many, like the BBC, provide chatrooms that concentrate on issues of topical interest or host online forums as a variation on chatrooms. If you are a Radio 1 fan, visit *www.bbc.co.uk/radio1/chat/*. If you watch Newsround visit *http://news.bbc.co.uk/cbbcnews/hi/chat/default.stm*. The BBC also publishes a guide to safe chatting at *www.bbc.co.uk/chatguide/*.

Which? Online hosts a forum where you can get expert advice on a range of topics and give others the benefit of your experience. For example, someone wrote in asking if anyone had travelled to

Australia and New Zealand as he and his family were considering their next holiday destination. There were lots of useful replies from people who had experienced those countries first-hand, as well as a list of suggested websites to visit, links to the *Holiday Which?* report on New Zealand and a 'virtual tour' website of Australia, which contained links to all sorts of information.

Instant messaging

If you don't fancy the idea of chatting in public just yet, you could use one of the messaging programs that allow you to have instant online private conversations with another person. Instant messages are a wonderful way to strike up spontaneous conversation with friends and family in far-flung places. You won't be alone in this pastime: over half of the people who use the Internet already use instant messaging as a way of keeping in touch.

The four most popular programs are AOL Messenger (with 49 per cent of users), MSN Messenger (29 per cent), Yahoo! Messenger (16 per cent) and ICQ (6 per cent). All programs are free to download from the host website. The person you want to chat to also needs to download the same program as you because the different programs cannot talk to each other. However, an Instant Messaging program called Trillian (*www.trillian.cc/trillian/index.html*) will allow you to message someone using any one of the big four. This is a free program and so definitely worth a look.

How do I get started?

All you need to do to get going is to add the name and email address of your friend into a contact list within the messaging program. You can have the program notify you when your friend comes online and then if it's convenient you can strike up a conversation. Yahoo! Messenger shows online friends with a large yellow smiley face. To send a message you simply double-click on your friend's name and type your opening line. After you click 'Send' your friend should receive the message in an instant and he or she can reply. Yahoo! Messenger has lots of wonderful gimmicky things to entertain you such as the facility to change the message box background to falling hearts, cartoon characters or an underwater sea scene.

Case history

Bridget has a friend, Mark, who spent some time in England but recently returned to his home in Australia. Until a few months ago they regularly emailed each other using Yahoo's web-based email service. Then quite by chance one day, they happened to be online sending emails to each other at the same time when Mark asked Bridget if she had ever used Yahoo! Messenger. Bridget says 'Within two minutes I had downloaded the Messenger software, added Mark's name to my list and started an online conversation. I couldn't believe it, it was quick, easy and really good fun! Our conversation was a lot more relaxed than the more formal emails we had been writing. In fact, it was more like chatting to Mark from the same room.

'When Mark is online my PC makes a noise like someone knocking on a door. It's really nice to know that he is there (even if the sound makes me jump out of my skin!). Now that the clocks have gone back Mark is online more often at the same time and it's wonderful when the message screen buzzes into view. Sometimes I even send him a message while he's asleep because I know that as soon as he goes online in the morning his system will tell him that he has a message waiting.

'I've grown to know Mark better through instant messaging than I ever would have done using email. We chat on for ages about all sorts of things. I would recommend it to anyone!'

Web cameras

If you enjoy sending instant messages then you will probably get a real buzz out of using a web camera. Also known as a *webcam*, it is a small video camera that sits on top of your PC and transmits a live video recording to another PC somewhere in the world. It is an ideal way for relatives who live some distance away to see members of their family on a regular basis.

Cost and features

You can get a web camera for as little as £20, and if you are prepared to spend a little more you can get a camera that will double up as a digital camera that can be used for taking photos away from the PC. More and more webcams are also being used as security cameras for outside the home. One of the basic things to check is whether a camera has a built-in microphone. If not, and you want to have a voice conversation while you view, you will need to buy a separate microphone that plugs directly into your computer's sound card. To attach a web camera to your PC you will probably also need to plug it into a USB port. Check that your computer has one (most recent PCs will).

How do I use a webcam?

Webcams are usually very easy to install and use. There are lots of Internet video-conferencing systems and messaging services around, such as Microsoft's NetMeeting, MSN Messenger and Yahoo! Messenger, that allow you to view live video over the Internet. All you have to do is to start the webcam and invite someone on your contact list to view it. A small window will appear on your screen showing you the image being transmitted to the other person. If both of you have a webcam, you will be able to see each other at the same time.

You can use a webcam through other software. In October 2001 *Which?* published a review of a system called Elive2U which sets up a video link between yourself and someone you are emailing. To use Elive2U you need to attach a microphone and webcam to your PC and then download software from the Elive2U site at *www.elive2u.com*. Before committing to buying the software (currently around £30), try downloading it for a free trial period and make sure you are happy with its performance.

Once you have downloaded the software, you have to send an email to the person with whom you want to have the video chat. The email contains a program that kicks into action as soon as the recipient opens his or her mail and enables him or her to see and hear you, live on video. Your friend can click on an icon and launch into a real-time text-based chat. If he or she wants to take part in a two-way chat on video, he or she will also need to download the software and attach a web camera and microphone to his or her PC. The *Which?* team reported no problems with downloading the software, installing it and getting it running, but felt that anyone other than a technical user might have difficulties with setting up a two-way link. Tests carried out by *Which?* also showed that the higher the PC specification and the faster the Internet connection, the smoother the picture and sound transmission were.

Although it can be really nice to talk to a live image on your computer screen, don't expect the same quality picture that you normally see on a TV. As the image is being transmitted down the phone line there can be delays in the speed with which it is delivered. This can result in jerky images, but you can get used to it just like you adjust to the time delays when you speak to someone from the other side of the world on the telephone. Clearly, if you have a broadband connection you will have a much better experience than with a slower Internet connection.

Case history

Robert and Katie have a young son, Tom. They use a webcam on a fairly regular basis so that their parents, who live a little way away, can watch him grow and change. 'It is brilliant for my parents,' says Robert. 'They were amongst the first to see Tom's new teeth and to watch him crawl around the room. It's great to see their faces light up when they watch him doing something for the first time! They feel a lot more involved than other grandparents in a similar position.'

Internet phones

With the right set-up you can use the Internet to make phone calls. This involves using Internet technology to send and receive digital voice data rather than sending voice messages down a normal phone line. Although the end result is the same, in that you can talk to someone using another PC connected to the Internet, there are some subtle differences. For a start, both parties need to install software that can handle voice calls, both need to have full-duplex sound cards so that they can talk and listen at the same time (although most new PCs have these soundcards already installed) and both need to invest in a good-quality microphone and speakers. You need to take some other factors into consideration. The quality of voice data is still rather poor and the speed of transmitting across the Net depends on the speed of your Internet connection and the amount of traffic on the Net at the time.

However, in spite of the current drawbacks, if you regularly speak to people in other countries, the cost of sending voice messages over the Internet can be a fraction of the cost of traditional international telephone calls. Internet calls should cost you only the price of a local call to your ISP.

The world of communications is also moving on at a rapid pace. You can now buy a WebPhone that contains all the software and equipment you need. All you have to do is to plug it into your PC, make sure the other person is online and make the call. Some web phone services already allow you to connect to a normal phone (see *www.callserve.com*).

Usenet

If you are the type of person who would shy away from entering a chatroom but would still welcome the opportunity to be involved in lively debate, then a part of the Internet known as Usenet may just be the thing for you. Usenet consists of over 60,000 newsgroups, discussion groups and bulletin boards and allows you to share ideas on virtually any topic you can think of. Some of the more popular newsgroups attract a large number of contributors, while others appeal only to a minority audience. The subject matter of the group also affects the nature of the discussions that will take place. Some newsgroups are academic or professional in nature and can be a source of valuable information, while others are light-hearted to say the least.

How do newsgroups work?

The concept is a simple one. Someone types a message and posts it up to the newsgroup server. Everyone in the group can see the message on their screen along with any replies that are posted. In theory, you should be able to follow the thread of a discussion around the particular topic being debated.

Who can take part?

Newsgroups are open to anyone and everyone. There is no restriction on who can post a message or reply to someone else's message.

Newsgroup categories

A Usenet site divides its newsgroups into major categories. Some of the common top-level categories are:

rec.   Hobbies, sports, games
alt.   Alternative discussions
talk.   Topical issues
biz.   Business services, reviews
sci.   Applied science, social science
news.   Usenet news

Within the science category you will find lots of sub-categories listed, along with the number of groups associated with each, such as sci.aeronautics, sci.astrology, sci.psychology and sci.space. When you find an interesting newsgroup you can choose to read a range of articles written around a subject area. If you want to visit a particular newsgroup on a regular basis, you can subscribe to it. Your newsreader will then make it easy for you to access the newsgroup, maybe by placing it high up on the list of newsgroups or grouping together all the newsgroups you subscribe to.

How do I get started?

To be able to follow or contribute to a newsgroup discussion, you need a special piece of software known as a *newsreader*. Fortunately, the two main web browsers, Internet Explorer and Netscape Navigator, both have newsreaders, which will give you access to most newsgroups. You will probably need to tell your newsreader the name of the news server used by your ISP. If you need help with this, contact your ISP. The newsreader will then download a list of all newsgroups from your ISP. You can also access newsgroups through the Net. Visit Google at *http://groups.google.com/* for a good place to start. Alternatively try *http://tile.net/* or *www.liszt.com/*.

Before you launch in, you would do well to read the Frequently Asked Questions (FAQ) section of the newsgroup and a couple of weeks' worth of postings. This will give you a good idea of the topics already explored by the group and the extent to which they have been covered. It should also help you to gauge the types of questions and answers that would be considered appropriate by the

group. Although most people who use Usenet are tolerant and helpful, some are less considerate and will have no qualms about putting you straight if they feel that you are wasting their time. At the very least, take your time before joining in with a discussion. You can sit on the sidelines (known as *lurking*) and read a discussion without anyone knowing that you are there.

There is a Usenet newsgroup called *news.newusers.questions* that contains excellent information about newsgroups and will probably answer any questions that you might have. This is a *moderated* newsgroup, which means that all postings are read before being made public.

Posting

You can either post a new article or reply to an existing one. Posting is similar to sending an email. If you are posting an article, make sure that your subject line reflects the content of your article so that you reach the right audience. If you are replying to an article, your newsreader will probably insert the original article in the reply. Delete those bits that are not significant to your reply. If you want to give it a go, consider posting your first reply to a test site such as *misc.test* or *alt.test*. Real users won't get to see your efforts but you will receive a reply from one of the sites that monitor these groups. If you want to try it out on real people, you could try *soc.penpals*.

And beware, if you post something that other people find distasteful, you may well find yourself the target of a *flame*. A flame is the Usenet equivalent of a spat or argument. Some newsgroups have been specially set up for flame wars.

Things to watch out for

As with any form of communication over the Net you never know whom you will meet or who may be collecting information about you. You can protect yourself to some degree, by following a few simple rules:

- always read the FAQ section of a newsgroup before you post a reply
- be polite and considerate of others
- don't post offensive material
- if your newsreader asks for your email address and signature (some take it directly from your Internet account), make up a false address. This will at least prevent those companies that trawl the Net looking for email addresses from hitting on a genuine account
- avoid getting drawn into get-rich-quick schemes.

Mailing lists

More and more people are using mailing lists as a way of keeping up with what's happening. If you subscribe to an online newsgroup, magazine or technical journal, your email will be added to a long list of other subscribers. Each time there is an update to a piece of information a message will be sent to everyone in the group. Mailing lists use email as the chief way of communicating with the group and so tend to be more accessible and easier to use than newsgroups. Many people also prefer the mailing list culture to the newsgroup culture, finding it less specialised and technical and more suitable for a general audience.

Finding people

Many of us think back to friends that we have known in the past and regret having lost touch with them. It may be that you were particularly friendly with someone at school or someone you once worked with. Maybe you have lost touch with someone in your family or would like to trace someone who worked with you. The Internet can be very useful in tracking down people.

People-finder sites

Although you may not be aware of it, a huge amount of information about each of us is in the public domain: in census records, birth and marriage details, employment records, entries in telephone directories, and of course what we enter each time we register with a website. Most people-finder sites work by building up individual profiles from information that they amalgamate from some of these sources.

Despite the range of information available, tracking someone down can be a frustrating and time-consuming process as there is currently no one central database containing all of this information. To some extent, the success of your search is dependent on the person you are trying to trace. You are likely to get more fruitful results if they have:

- posted their email address to a website at some time (search engines look for names and email addresses found on web pages)
- registered details with a people-finder search engine
- taken part in an online discussion or email discussion list
- registered with an online ISP which has recorded their email address.

Most people-finder sites require you to register your details before they will allow you to search. This is their way of including your details in the database that they are building. It probably also goes without saying, but the more information you have about someone, the more likely you are to find him or her. For example, if you are searching for Jon Green but don't know where he lives or what year he was at college with you, you are probably in for a long haul!

Many sites concentrate on finding people in the USA so if you want to find someone in the UK you need to access a UK site. Some sites collect information from international sources. *www.worldemail. com* is one such site. It claims to have access to millions of email addresses around the world. You could also try *www.peoplesearch.net*, which has access to international people-search facilities, or *www.192.com*, which claims to be the largest directory service in the UK (its name represents the number that was used for directory services). Its database includes over 45 million people on the electoral register for 2001 and 13 million people from the Directory Enquiries database. You will need to enter a location before it can search.

If you don't find what you want through specific sites, try using a search engine to search for **finding people +UK** or something similar. The list will include sites that specialise in adoption cases, detective agencies who offer to track down unfaithful partners, or people who owe you money, as well dating agencies. Most sites that carry out detailed or specialised searches charge a fee, so before you sign up, read the site's terms and conditions very carefully.

FriendsReunited

FriendsReunited (*www.friendsreunited.co.uk*), a much-talked about site, began in 1999 when Julie Pankhurst was pregnant and wondered what her old school friends were up to. In just a few years the site has achieved phenomenal success, which just goes to show how many people are interested in finding old friends and colleagues.

The FriendsReunited website is designed to put you in touch with old friends. It boasts a database of over 40,000 secondary and primary schools, colleges and universities and currently has the details for more than 8 million people. The membership rate is said to be increasing at over 15,000 people per day. Future developments of the site include building on the number of people that can be located via their place of work or through membership of teams and clubs. To date, 2 million people have registered details for their place of work and the site has information for over 150,000 ex-servicemen and women.

How it works

FriendsReunited does not charge for registering your details. Your name can appear in a list associated with your school, university, place of work and so on. You are allowed to receive unlimited emails and voice messages and read other people's details. The cost of full membership is £7.50 for the first year, and £5 for renewing it. For this you will be able to send as many voice and email messages as you want to other members, post photos on a message board and put reunion and other school details on the website.

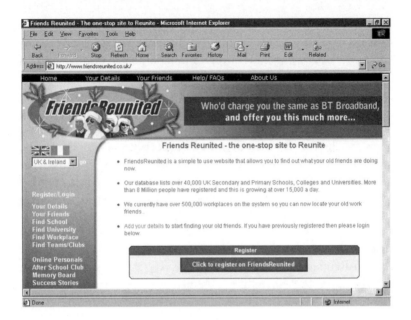

Case history

Hilary is 43 years old and recently went to a sixth form reunion held at her high school. She hadn't seen many of her friends for 25 years.

'It was one of the best experiences of this year. A couple of boys from my sixth form got together about 12 months ago and decided that they would organise a reunion. Although they lived near London and we went to school in Warrington, they were still in touch with a few people. Between them they managed to come up with a fair few names and telephone numbers but, as you might expect, there were still a lot of people missing. They put a notice out on FriendsReunited and the numbers started snowballing. They set up their own website and posted old school photos on it, along with lots of funny things that people remembered from years back. They booked a buffet dinner and a 1970s disco through the Internet. Although they didn't find everyone through FriendsReunited they felt sure that there wouldn't have been a reunion without it.'

People Tracer

Peopletracer UK (*www.peopletracer.net*) was formed in 1997 as an online agency for reuniting family and friends and claims to be able to access a database containing 45 million names and 27 million addresses for people in the UK. It also maintains that of the 4,000 enquiries processed last year, 85 per cent were successful. As well as reuniting friends and family, this site is aimed at those who are actively seeking people they may never have met, such as birth parents, adopted children or siblings. For £25 you can commission a basic report, which will provide information that matches criteria you have submitted. It is then up to you what you do with the information and how you proceed with finding the person you are looking for. For £35 you can receive an advanced report that provides you with names of co-habitants and telephone numbers. If you want to take it further you can pay a non-refundable fee of £125 to cover administration and research costs and a further £125 if the team actually locates the person for you.

Missing persons

If you want to try to find a missing person, the site of the National Missing Persons Helpline (a charity dedicated to helping missing people and their families) provides a useful vehicle. It can be found at *www.missingpersons.org/*. Alternatively, try Search UK at *www.search-uk.org*.

University or college friends

If you want to find university or college friends try *www.roastbeef.co.uk*. Find your university, register your details and then view the member lists or put a message on a message board. You can even chat in a virtual student bar.

E-cards

If you've forgotten to mail a card for someone's birthday and don't think an email is special enough, you could send an e-card. Try the free greetings cards available through *www.yahoo.com* or *www.123greetings.com*. Simply select a category or card, type your message, fill in details of your email address and that of the person to whom you are sending the card and send it. Many of the cards are animated and play music when they are opened by the recipient.

Blue Mountain (*www.bluemountain.com*) also has an extensive range of e-cards, including categories for different religious celebrations and cards designed to appeal to teenagers or extended family members, but you have to pay to send most of them. Paid-up members can choose to send any card on the site as many times as they wish. Membership currently costs $13.95 per year. The benefits of membership include two free accounts for friends or family, setting up reminders for special events and the ability to attach a digital photo to a card.

Chapter 7

Shopping

For some, shopping is a pleasure. Searching out bargains, trying on clothes, even window-shopping, can prove an enjoyable way to spend an afternoon. For others shopping is a necessary evil, something to be avoided at all costs. But for the majority, there is a middle ground. Some shopping is pleasurable and some a tiresome chore. This is where shopping online can come into its own, you can be selective and tailor it to your preferences. You may be happy to buy books, CDs and the weekly groceries online but want to buy electrical goods and clothes from the high street. The choice is yours. Although shopping on the Internet can be frustrating, it can certainly save you both time and money.

Finding shops online

Some of the most interesting shops to be found on the Internet are those that you have probably never heard of. These shops are purely 'virtual' – they do not have any 'bricks and mortar' outlets. You will also find many of the familiar high street names providing an online shopping service. In most cases the products listed mirror those available in the store – on some sites you have less choice and on a few you may find more items online than in the store.

Where to start

Finding what you want online can prove a daunting task. The best starting point is personal recommendation. Ask your friends and family if they have come across any sites that have proved easy to use, reliable and cost effective. Keep a note of the website addresses and give them a try. Alternatively, look at the site of a shop that you are familiar with and trust, such as Marks and Spencer. It is usually quite easy to guess the website address of well-known shops and companies, or you can find the address on their marketing literature. Failing that, use a search engine such as *www.google.com* or *www.yahoo.com* (see Chapter 2 for details on how to search) to search for sites offering specific goods.

Internet portals

Many Internet Service Providers (ISPs) and larger search engines run their own 'portal' sites that include shopping sections. Portal sites have been designed to offer a one-stop shop for all your Internet needs, providing services such as news, weather, magazine articles, chat forums as well as access to a range of shopping sites. The aim is to attract you to use the portal as a starting point when you use the Internet. Such portal sites usually offer a limited range of retailers who have paid a premium to have their site included. This has its advantages and disadvantages. The fact that you have a manageable list of sites can prove beneficial, especially if the portal site has evaluated and vetted the customer service provided by these sites. On the other hand, if you always stay within the confines of the portal site your online shopping experience will be limited and you will not experience the vast choice available on the Net.

Microsoft provides a popular portal site (*www.msn.co.uk*) incorporating a number of shopping categories. Each category provides a choice of between two and eight retailers, including some major high street names such as Littlewoods, Tesco and PC World.

Shopping directories

Shopping directories are sites that provide links to a range of shopping-related sites. They are usually divided into categories of products and services to make it easier to find what you are looking for. As with portal sites, you will move directly to the website of the retailer once you have clicked on a link. Shopping directories can provide links to thousands of shops as well as related services such as price-comparison, auction and co-buying sites. Some can be overwhelming, others restrictive. It is very much a case of finding one that suits you.

The better directories will vet the sites included and provide a description that points out strengths and weaknesses. Try *The Guardian*'s *http://shopping.guardian.co.uk* site, which has reviews of sites, is easy to use and covers unusual as well as run-of-the-mill sites and products. Alternatively, try *www.britishcompanies.co.uk* or *www.uk250. co.uk*. The UK 250 site provides links to a range of outlets from Harvey Nichols (*www.harveynichols.com*) to Matalan (*www.matalan.co.uk*).

Getting a good deal

Shopping on the Internet is all about convenience, but it is important to make sure that you are not paying over the odds by shopping from home. The following sections will show you how you can secure a good deal.

Price-comparison sites

Price-comparison sites are an essential first port of call for any shopper who knows exactly what he or she wants and wishes to get the best price. These sites search the Internet for the best deals for the products you request. They often list prices from the online stores, high street retailers as well as auction and buying groups. In some cases this is extremely successful but on other occasions it may prove less helpful. In general, it depends on what you are searching for: price comparisons on common items such as CDs will usually provide accurate like-for-like comparisons, whereas it is often more difficult to find true comparisons for more unusual items or those with detailed specifications. However, they are worth a try. Remember that sites that pay to advertise on the comparison sites are normally listed at the top of your search results.

Tip

As well as the dedicated price-comparison sites, many of the shopping directory and portal sites also include a comparison facility. It is worth bearing in mind that many of these price-comparison facilities will search for prices only on affiliated sites. You are unlikely to get a true comparison across the entire market. It is worth searching using more than one comparison site and supplementing your research with a couple of phone calls to high street retailers for special deals.

In the main, price-comparison sites have a similar look and feel. The first step is usually to select the category of product that you are looking to buy. You then enter details of the product and initiate the search. The site should provide a number of outlets that stock the item with details of price and delivery charge. Try the following three sites and compare the results for an identical item (*http://uk.pricerunner.com*, *www.priceguideuk.com* and *www.dealtime.co.uk*). Although you may find that one site consistently offers you the best price, it is always advisable to try at least a couple of sites before you buy. It is also worth considering a price-comparison site that specialises in just one type of product. If you are looking for books for example, a search on *www.bookbrain.co.uk* may find you a bargain.

For a wider range of price-comparison sites use a search engine and search on the words 'price comparison'. Make sure that you are searching the entire web and not just UK sites (there is usually a box to check). The resulting list will include non-UK sites, giving you the opportunity to compare UK prices with those in the USA.

Tip

Check whether the price comparisons include VAT, delivery charges and, if buying from abroad, import tax. You will not be able to make a true comparison unless all prices are like for like.

Case history

Shana uses the Internet to buy books on a fairly regular basis. She has always used Amazon (*www.amazon.co.uk*), believing it to be the cheapest option. A colleague told her about price-comparison sites and she decided to try one before placing her next order.

'I guess I use Amazon out of habit and I had always assumed that I wouldn't find books cheaper anywhere else on the Net. I know that the postage pushes up the price and I could probably find it cheaper in a bookshop but as I'm not often in town I'm happy to pay a bit extra for the convenience.

'I was looking for a particular title on three price-comparison sites and the results were mixed to say the least! One couldn't find

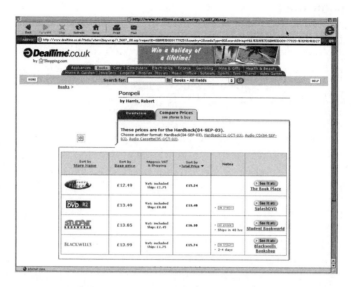

it at all even with the title and ISBN number, another said it was out of print, but Deal Time did manage to track it down for me at four outlets.

'Unfortunately, Amazon wasn't one of the included sites so I accessed the site independently and found that the book was available and cheaper, so I ended up using Amazon yet again.'

Auction sites

Online auctions provide a forum for individuals who want to buy or sell items and also for retailers who need to offload surplus stock. They have become extremely popular with those participating and those who simply enjoy watching the race.

Most auction sites operate in a similar way. Items for sale are usually divided into categories that can be all-encompassing or specialised, depending on the site. In most cases you will be free to browse without registering, but once you decide to bid you will need to provide your credit-card details. Most sites provide the option to browse all the items within a category or search within the site for a specific requirement. Auction sites are usually quite easy to navigate and the best way to become familiar with the way they work is to have a go. Try *www.qxl.com* or *www.ebay.co.uk* as a starting point.

Once something catches your eye, the next step is to place your bid. You need to make an offer that is higher than the currently displayed bid. You need to keep a watchful eye as it is quite likely that the original bidder or a new player will outbid you. The auction site sets a time limit that is usually displayed beside the item details in days and hours. When the specified time is reached, the auction site or the individual seller will notify the highest bidder.

Placing the highest bid does not necessarily mean that you get the item. Some items have a reserve price and if that price is not reached the item is withdrawn from the auction when the time expires.

If you are unable to keep track of the bidding process yourself, set a maximum bid and ask the auction site to outbid any other offers until it reaches your maximum (you usually specify an increment to increase your bid by, say, £10). If counterbids fall short of your specified maximum you will pay only one increment above the last counterbid. Alternatively, if you enjoy the chase, you can ask the auction site to email you if someone has outbid you.

Although auction sites can provide hours of fun, it is important to be aware that they can legally refuse to accept responsibility for the quality of the goods they auction. In practice, many of the larger auction sites do offer extra guarantees or free insurance and it is worth reading the small print before you commit yourself. It is also worth noting that this extra protection does not always extend to purchases from an individual (as opposed to the site itself), and you may not have the same protection if something goes wrong. If the goods are faulty, not as advertised or simply do not arrive you may find it difficult to get your money back.

Case history

Carl is most definitely an online auction convert. Until a few months ago he didn't even know what an auction site was but now he admits to having a quick look almost on a daily basis.

'The first time I placed a bid online I didn't know what to expect. I'd just bought a new laptop computer but had decided not to splash out the extra £50 for a carrying case. Once it arrived I realised my mistake. I was just about to order one when a colleague mentioned that he had found a bargain case through the auction site eBay (*www.ebay.co.uk*). I went online that evening and found it easy to find my way around the site. There was plenty of helpful information for those new to auction sites.

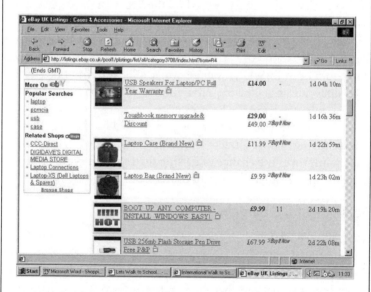

'I soon found what I was looking for – in fact, I had a choice of two. By clicking on the picture I could find out more details such as size, delivery details and postage costs. In this instance I didn't need to bid as the item had a 'Buy it now' flag. This means that you can commit to pay the quoted price and the item will be posted out to you straight away. I think it must have been a shop or dealer selling the bags as they had 15 for sale. There was also a list of comments from satisfied customers that helped to put my mind at rest. In all the bag cost me £16.99, including £5 postage and it arrived three days later!

'Since then I have become more adventurous and have bid for quite a few items. I think my best bargain was a nearly new tent that cost just £20. I have seen a similar one in a shop for £80.'

Group-buying sites

The idea behind this type of site is to buy in bulk and attract discounts. The site will approach a company and negotiate a deal based on a bulk purchase. For example, it may approach an electrical wholesaler and agree a per-item price based on buying 1,000 toasters. The toaster is then advertised on the site with the expected discount price should 1,000 orders be placed. A time limit is usually stipulated. If you place your order you will get your toaster at the stated price as soon as 1,000 orders are placed. The downside is that you could be in for a long wait or, worse still, you may find that the offer does not attract the required number of purchasers and you do not get your toaster at the bargain price.

Let's Buy It (*www.letsbuyit.com*) is probably the best-known group-buying site. It attracts buyers from all over Europe, which greatly improves the chance of netting the required number of participants in a reasonable amount of time.

Searching for a bargain

Most shoppers love a bargain, but with thousands of shops of both the traditional and online variety to scour, it can be a thankless task. Sites such as *www.unbeatable.co.uk* are designed to help. It tracks down bargains that can then be purchased from the high street. It will also track auctions, end of lines, returns and slightly damaged electrical goods. The Bargains site (*www.bargains.co.uk*) also provides some tempting cut-price offers.

For a wider choice of sites, use a search engine and enter the search words 'bargain shopping'. You should find plenty of choice, including price-comparison sites as well as sites scouring the high street shops and mail-order outlets. Last but not least, for a real bargain, take a look at *www.freeinuk.co.uk*. This site searches out items that are absolutely free – and you can't get a better bargain than that!

Tip

Many bargain-hunting sites notify you if the bargain you are searching for comes up. It is worth checking whether this is an option with your favourite site.

Safe online shopping

Many of the horror stories regarding online shopping are grossly exaggerated. Isolated incidents such as credit-card fraud, private details being exposed on the Net and goods that never arrive are newsworthy and often receive excessive media coverage. In reality, when you shop online you face the same pitfalls and pleasures as you do with any other shopping experience. Customers have the same rights when buying online as they do when using mail order or when purchasing goods from traditional shops. Equally, shoppers, regardless of the medium, need to minimise risks by taking sensible precautions. The sections below give details of steps you can take to ensure that your online shopping experiences are trouble-free.

Protection for online shoppers

Credit-card payments

A survey by *Which?* in March 2001 found that although more than 3 million British adults claim to shop online, one in four considered that they are taking a risk using a credit card. There is a popular misconception that shopping online poses more risks than conventional methods such as mail order and face-to-face shopping. In fact, the majority of credit-card fraud results from discarded paper receipts picked up by unscrupulous people from the street or in supermarkets. It is true to say that once your credit-card details have fallen into the wrong hands it is relatively easy for them to be used anonymously when purchasing goods by telephone or over the Internet. However, the majority of credit-card fraud still takes place on the high street using stolen or forged cards, with only a small percentage linked to Internet fraud.

Paying by credit card is a sensible move when buying any goods over a distance, whether by mail order or online. In the unusual event of your credit card being used fraudulently, you are entitled to a full refund from your credit-card company. This provides better protection than high street transactions, where you are usually liable for the first £50 of any claim. Of course, you need to realise that your card has been used without your knowledge before you can claim. It is always worth checking your credit-card statements carefully and making sure that all transactions can be accounted for. If you do notice any discrepancies, contact the company that issued your card immediately.

Consumer rights

UK law states that all goods sold must be fit for purpose, of a satisfactory quality, match their description and be safe to use. This applies however you shop. If the goods you buy do not meet these criteria you are entitled to your money back. If you have paid by credit card you can claim your money back from the card company for goods costing between £100 and £30,000.

The law protects all consumers, but there are additional safeguards for those purchasing over a distance (where you don't see the seller face to face). Distance Selling Regulations provide the following assurances:

- the right to a refund if your card is used fraudulently
- a cooling-off period of seven working days, during which you can change your mind and cancel the order
- orders to be confirmed by the seller in writing (or by fax/email) and be delivered within 30 days
- the retailer to provide a geographical address in addition to an email address
- the retailer to keep all information about you secure.

The regulations do provide for some flexibility for retailers. For example, the stipulated delivery period may not be practical for goods made to your specifications or for goods that are perishable, such as flowers or food. There are also some goods that cannot be returned if they have been opened, such as shrink-wrapped CDs or videos. If you are unsure, you can always check at the Office of Fair Trading website (*www.oft.gov.uk/consumer*).

Buying from a non-European Union site can prove more complicated (see *Buying from abroad*). Some credit-card companies will not provide a refund for goods purchased from non-UK sites. It is worth checking with your credit-card company that you are covered.

Secure sites

If you are purchasing any goods online it is important to check the site's security policy. Secure sites use something known as secure socket layer technology (SSL) to keep your confidential information away from prying eyes. Confidential information that you enter, such as your personal details and credit-card number, are encrypted. The characters are scrambled using a mathematical formula, sent down the phone line and then unscrambled at the other end. Sometimes sites will have a few pages that are secure rather than being fully secure. In this case, you are usually told that you are entering a secure page when you are required to enter personal information. You can identify a secure site in two ways:

- the web address will begin https:// rather than the standard http://. The inclusion of the letter 's' indicates that it is a secure site
- the site or pages on it will have a picture of a closed padlock or an unbroken key, usually at the bottom of the screen. If you hold your mouse over this symbol you will be able to determine the level of security. Online banks usually use an encryption level of 128 whereas 40 is the normal encryption level for shopping sites.

If a site stores your personal details it should ensure that they remain encrypted while stored and be held behind a firewall (a security measure that protects sensitive information held on any computer that is linked to the Internet). Companies without this protection should not hold personal data.

Some of the more high-profile Internet news stories have involved people accessing confidential information over the Internet. In most cases this has been down to an error on the part of an employee of the company or software problems rather than the overall security measures in place.

Protecting yourself

Even if the law protects you, dealing with fraud can be distressing and time-consuming. It is worth taking some simple steps to minimise your risk. Once you have found a site that you want to buy from, use the following checklist before you part with your credit-card details.

- Check that the site has a security policy, and read the terms and conditions carefully.
- Make sure that you can contact the retailer by some means other than email, such as a phone number or address.
- Do not send any confidential information without being confident that the site is secure.
- Keep copies of any emails to do with the transaction. If you do not receive a confirmation of your order, ask for one.
- Check your credit-card statements carefully.
- Do not include any confidential information, such as credit-card details, in an email.
- Remember to uncheck the box that gives your permission for the site to pass on your details. If you don't do this you are likely to receive a mass of junk emails.

Tip

For added peace of mind, look for traders who adhere to a specific code of practice. TrustUK (*www.trustuk.org.uk*) was set up to develop standards for web trading and approve online codes of practice. Check on its site to find out the codes of practice endorsed by the scheme.

Buying from abroad

There is nothing to prevent a UK citizen buying goods online from another country. In fact, the opportunity to buy goods from anywhere in the world is exactly what makes shopping on the Internet so amazing. Some goods may be cheaper, but the real attraction has to be the diversity and variety of goods suddenly at your fingertips. But, before you get too carried away, it is worth considering some of the possible drawbacks.

Payment considerations

Some foreign sites do not deliver abroad and those that do may not accept credit cards issued in another country. This can be the case with sites in the USA – many either do not accept cards issued outside of the USA or will accept only American Express cards. You may find that you can wire money or send travellers cheques, but if you do, you lose the legal comeback you have with a credit-card purchase should something go wrong.

Working out the cost
Prices will be quoted in the currency of the country selling the goods. Sites such as *www.xe.com/ucc* provide handy currency-conversion tables to help you with this.

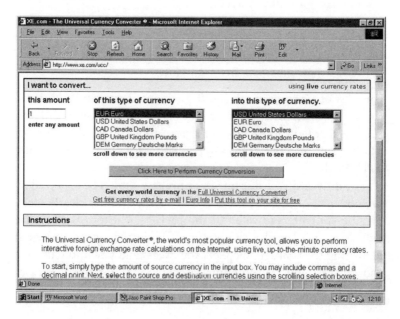

Once you have worked out the price in sterling the next step is to consider whether any additional tariffs apply. In many cases the delivery charge will be in addition to the quoted price. You may be offered a choice of methods of delivery, some quicker and more expensive than others. Add the delivery charge to the cost and check that you cannot get a better deal from a UK site or the high street.

If you are purchasing goods from the European Union (EU) you will probably need to pay VAT on top of the quoted price. If you are buying from outside of the EU you are likely to be liable for duty as well as VAT. For example, you will need to pay 14 per cent import duty plus 17.5 per cent VAT on a camcorder purchased from the USA. The VAT due on the purchase is calculated after the duty has been added. These additional costs can often make the goods more expensive than buying locally.

There are some general rules, but VAT and duty levels do vary and they are not payable on all purchases, so it is worth checking. At the time of writing:

- alcohol, tobacco and perfumes are always liable for duty and VAT
- goods that cost less than £18 (including post and packaging) are not liable for duty or VAT
- books are duty- and VAT-free, making them a popular foreign purchase
- computers, computer parts and digital cameras (the still variety rather than video) are free from duty.

For a list of common items and the associated duty and VAT rates, check the Customs and Excise website (*www.hmce.gov.uk*). If you need further help, telephone its Advice Service on (0845) 010 9000. The website also provides examples of how to calculate the duty and VAT due.

The duty and VAT due on your purchase should be collected by the postman or delivery service. The retailer should clearly identify the contents and value of the package. Customs and Excise will then calculate the excess due. It is then down to the agent delivering the package to collect the excess and pay it to Customs and Excise. There is sometimes a charge for this. In some cases purchasers escape paying any duty or VAT simply because no one asks them for it.

Advice for buying from abroad

- Find out how returns are handled (in case you have a problem with the purchase and need to send it back) and who pays the postage. If you are liable to bear the cost it could make it an expensive non-purchase.
- If you are buying electrical equipment make sure you find out if you will be supplied with a compatible power supply.
- Make sure the guarantee is valid in the UK.
- Be careful when buying videos from abroad: those from the USA and Japan are NTSC format and cannot be played on UK VHS recorders. Also, unless you own a multi-region DVD player, take care when purchasing DVDs because they are region-specific.

Online shopping – step by step

Shopping online can be a delight or it can have you pulling your hair out in frustration – much the same as shopping in the high street. The knack is to find sites where customer service meets, or exceeds, your expectations. Invariably there will be an element of trial and error, but stick with it – once you have found some good sites you will never look back.

Ordering online

Once you have found what you are looking for and checked out the site's security and terms and conditions, you are ready to place your order. No two online shops are exactly the same but there are similarities. With most sites you click on the item you want to buy and then you 'add the item to your to shopping basket, usually by clicking on an icon of a shopping basket' or similar. When you have made all your selections you 'proceed to the checkout' by clicking on a checkout icon of some form. You may now be presented with a list of all your purchases and the total price (some sites provide this information only once you have entered your personal details). There is usually the opportunity to take out any unwanted items or go back to the shop to purchase additional items. Once you are happy with your final choices you confirm your order. At this point you may be informed that you are entering a secure page and you will be asked to type in your personal details and credit-card number.

The ordering process can be simplified if you are a regular purchaser from the site. Some sites will keep your personal details on file so that you do not have to type them in each time you place an order. If this is the case, you will need to log in and provide a password for identification.

Case history

On her own admission, Isabel doesn't use the Internet very often for shopping. She describes herself as a tactile person and she likes to see and feel something before parting with her money.

'I can't understand how people can buy vegetables or fruit over the Internet, although I guess I can see the advantages of buying staple-packaged groceries. And how people buy clothes and shoes online, or by mail-order for that matter, beats me! But one thing I do organise online is sending flowers. Even if you go to a florist and send flowers (by Interflora) you don't actually see what you are buying so you may as well skip the middle man.

'I use Interflora (*www.interflora.co.uk*) – it seems to have plenty of choice and has always been reliable. I usually first look at the

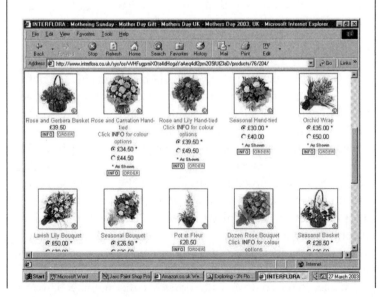

---

seasonal choices, clicking on the 'Info' button if there is something I like the look of.

'To place the order I click on the 'Order' button and it takes me through to a secure page. You can either register if you have used the site before, or add your details if you are a new customer.

'The padlock at the bottom of the screen shows you that the site is secure. And on this site you actually have to check the box if you want to be added to the mailing list, which makes a refreshing change! You then enter the details of the person receiving the flowers, provide your credit-card details and the order is placed. Interflora will send an email to confirm your order which is always reassuring.'

Some sites will also remember your preferences or details of your previous orders. Supermarket sites will often allow you to see your last order or even a list of everything you have ever ordered. You can then use this as a starting point for your new order, deleting the items you do not require and selecting additional items from the online store.

Case history

Mary had recently been widowed and, not having driven for many years, was finding trips to the supermarket increasingly stressful. Her son suggested that she shop online. He helped her set up an account with Asda (*www.asda.co.uk*) and she has not looked back since. In fact since then she has also set up an account with Tesco (*www.tesco.com*).

'I'm not a computer buff and I was nervous about using the Internet but it was the lesser of two evils. I hated the drive to the nearest town and there is only a newsagent in my village so I had no choice – I have to eat!

'I tend to use the Tesco site more – it's just personal preference. Both the Asda and Tesco sites are easy to use and I've never had any problems with delivery.

'Once I'm on the site I have to log in and give my password.

'I then click on the 'Groceries' option on the left of the screen. I like this site because it remembers what I have bought before. I do a shop only about once a month and I usually want more or less the same things so it saves a lot of time if I can use my favourites as a starting point.

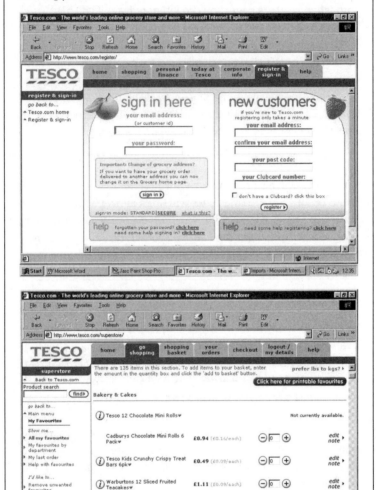

'Once I've gone through my favourites I click the 'Add to basket' button. I then usually look at the special offers and add anything

> that takes my fancy before clicking on the 'Checkout' button. Once at the checkout I pick a delivery time slot, usually the next day and I then type in my credit-card number. And that's it, easy!'

Many sites gather information on you as you browse their site and make purchases. This information is saved in a file known as a 'cookie' (see Chapter 2), which is placed on your browser. This has obvious marketing advantages for retailers as they can send you details of new products or offers that they think will be of interest. Equally, this can be of benefit to you as it can save you money and keep you up-to-date with new products. Some sites also use the information to make you feel welcome. For example, the Amazon site will remember your name and greet you personally when you next visit the site.

Tip

If you do not want cookies on your machine, you can reset your browser to disable or delete them. How you do this depends on the browser you have installed, but it is always straightforward (*www. cookiecentral.com* provides details). It may be worth noting that some sites will not allow you access if their cookies have been disabled.

Order confirmation

You should automatically receive an email from the site confirming your order. This confirmation will usually arrive promptly. If it does not, contact the site and ask for a confirmation. It is advisable to print a copy of this confirmation for your records. Then, in the event of a dispute, you have proof of the details of the order.

Delivery

The issues surrounding the delivery of goods bought from an Internet site are the same as those encountered when buying mail order. Most of the time the goods arrive without a hitch but occasionally you will come across problems.

Some sites state a maximum delivery time to cover themselves. So, although they state a 30-day delivery period, you may well receive the goods much sooner. The delivery period is likely to be much quicker if you are purchasing from a UK site. If you are in a hurry to receive the goods you will find that some sites will arrange next-day delivery, usually for an additional charge. Some sites deliver your goods by courier but the majority tend to use standard post or the Parcelforce service.

Details about delivery charges can sometimes be difficult to find on sites and, on some occasions, they are not presented until you have provided your credit-card details. You will also find that some sites waive the delivery charge. If this is the case, make sure that the goods are competitively priced – the delivery costs may have simply been hidden in the purchase price. If the site does not provide details of its delivery procedures either email or phone to find out.

Returning goods

You can send something back within seven days of delivery if you decide you do not want it. However, if the goods are not faulty you may find that you have to foot the bill for the postage, and this can be significant if the item is heavy. It is certainly worth reading the small print before you buy an item about which you are unsure. However, this may not always be possible because not all sites provide information on how to return unwanted or defective goods. If you cannot find the information online, it may be best to shop elsewhere.

Returning goods purchased online

If you have purchased an item from a website with a high street outlet you may be able to return the goods in person.

Only the buyer has the legal right to return an unwanted item, but some sites will allow you to return a gift in exchange for replacement goods or vouchers. In most cases refunds can be made only to the purchaser's credit cards. Millets and Argos are unusual in that they will refund to a third party if they can provide proof of purchase.

Sites usually have a time limit for returning unwanted goods. This is often extended over the Christmas period.

If the goods are faulty you should not have to pay for the return postage. However, some sites will not refund the delivery postage. A report by *Which?* in January 2003 found that around a third of the sites surveyed make you pay the delivery postage whether you keep the goods or not.

So what do you do if you don't get your money back? If you have paid by credit card you can claim the refund from the card company. Alternatively, you can contact the Office of Fair Trading (*www.oft.gov.uk*) for advice, or try the DTI's Consumer Gateway site *www.consumer.gov.uk*. The latter is the government's online Consumer Advice Centre, providing a wealth of advice for consumers for both online and offline purchases. For up-to-date reports, news and issues on consumers' rights try the Consumers' International site (*www.consumersinternational.org*).

Chapter 8

Travel

More and more people are using the Internet to organise travel. It is estimated that 39 million people in Western Europe booked their travel arrangements online in 2002. This was 25 per cent up on 2001, and amounted to online sales of €7.3 billion.

So, what are consumers happy to buy online? As you might expect, more money is spent booking flights than on any other aspect of travel (62 per cent of online sales as opposed to 12 per cent for hotels, 10 per cent for rail and 3 per cent for car hire). Of course, the Internet is much more than just a vehicle for making a booking. You can:

- compare prices
- compare routes and length of journeys
- get details of flight, rail or coach times, seating arrangements, car parking and trips
- read location guides
- get up-to-date travel and health information for any area of the world.

This chapter looks at how to make the most of what is available online whether you are travelling by air, rail, road or sea. Some of the general travel sites covered in the section on travelling by air also provide services for other forms of transport.

For general tips on how to buy online, see Chapter 7.

Air travel

The opening up of new, cheap routes has made continental Europe (and many destinations worldwide) much more accessible than ever before. You can search for the cheapest fare available on a date of your choice, and in theory in the time it would have taken you to read the brochures and visit the travel agent, you can make a booking, pick up your tickets online and be on your way.

No frills

Not surprisingly, the biggest take-up of online flights has been for low-cost, 'no frills' airlines – budget airlines that aim to get you to your destination as quickly and cheaply as possible. They have kept the cost to a minimum by operating a few select routes to and from cheaper airports throughout Europe. They have also cut down on some of the niceties that are part of the package with most scheduled airlines, such as inclusive meals and drinks.

The budget airlines include easyJet (*www.easyJet.com*), Ryanair (*www.ryanair.com*), MyTravelLite (*www.mytravellite.com*) and Virgin Express (*www.virginexpress.com*).

Although low-cost airlines have revolutionised the flight industry and opened up European travel, there are some drawbacks. As mentioned above, meals and drinks are not usually included in the price. Moreover, to get the best prices you generally have to book well in advance or take a chance and leave your arrangements to the very last minute. If you are travelling with children you may not end up with the bargain that you expect as children usually pay the same fare as adults. There may also be little choice over where you sit and what time of day you travel, and once you've made a booking, you might find that steep costs are involved if you want to make an alteration or cancel. Destination airports can sometimes be located well outside of the city that you are visiting, adding to your overall transport costs. Of course, some of these things will also be true of other airlines but as you are likely to be doing the leg-work yourself and may not go through a travel agent, the advice, as always, is to read the pricing structure, flight details and terms and conditions carefully to avoid disappointment.

Scheduled airlines

Although it would seem from the popularity of the no frills airlines that price is the overriding factor in deciding which airline to fly with, this is not always the case. Most people also expect a good standard of customer service. If service is important to you then you may be better off looking at some of the airlines that still offer the 'frills' as part of the package. These are traditionally airlines that operate scheduled flights, such as British Airways (*www. ba.com*), BMI (*www.flybmi.com*) and British European's Flybe (*www.flybe.com*).

BA promotes the fact that service is the one thing that makes it a cut above the rest. As you might expect from one of the airline giants, the BA site is well laid out and easy to use. Terms and conditions are readily available and easy to understand. The site also has lots of useful information such as daily flight news, arrivals and departures and so on. Although you may find cheaper deals if you shop around, there are compensations for choosing to book through a site like BA. You can email questions to the Customer Service team, who guarantee to get back to you within 24 hours; you can search through a comprehensive list of questions and answers; or enquire about an existing booking. Interestingly, BA now offers permanently low-cost flights to Europe.

Here is a summary of what you can expect from a scheduled airline.

Advantages	Disadvantages
You can get still get some exceedingly cheap fares.	Just like the 'no frills' airlines, cheap fares on the full-service airlines are usually available only if you book well in advance of the departure date, and prices usually go up the closer you get to the departure date.
They operate from central locations around the UK and destination airports are usually close to the city that you are visiting.	You may not be able to get discount fares for children.
Meals and drinks are usually included.	
To get a cheap deal you used to have to stay over a Saturday night, but BA, Flybe and BMI no longer stipulate this as a requirement on most European flights.	
They are likely to offer overnight accommodation if the last flight of the day is cancelled.	

If a cheap deal is what you are looking for, don't forget to check out some of the UK's charter companies as well as the scheduled airlines. Companies specialising in package holidays often charter their own planes and then sell off unfilled seats. At one time you could pick up only a reduced-price return ticket that was restricted to a fixed 7- or 14-night duration, but now companies like Air 2000 (*www.air2000.com*) and Britannia (*www.britanniadirect.com*) offer one-way tickets and more flexible lengths of stay.

How to choose a site

You can look on the website of individual airlines such as Singapore Airlines (*www.singaporeair.com*) or Qantas (*www.qantas.com.au*) to see what they have to offer. You will find a complete list of UK and international airlines on the A2bTravel website (*www.a2btravel.com*) and on the Airlines of the Web site (*www.flyaow.com/airlinehomepages.htm*).

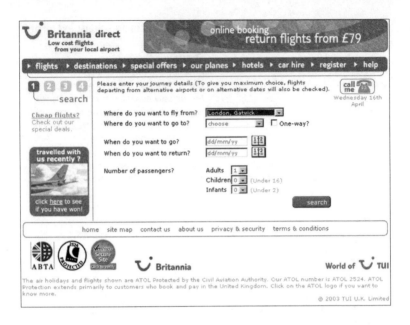

Once you have checked the price on the airline's site it is always worth searching a price-comparison site, consolidator site or general travel site before making a booking. And if you are feeling really brave, you could try your hand at a travel auction. All these options are briefly outlined below.

What type of site suits you best really depends on what your needs and preferences are. There are plenty of sites out there that you can explore until you settle on a few that save you money and make your life easy in the bargain. Use this checklist to help you decide what you want from a site.

Considerations	Site features
Price is the key issue	Does the site show prices prominently? Does it tell you upfront what extra charges you can expect to pay? Beware: many sites add tax late on in the booking process.
Online bookings	Not all sites let you book online, and you may have to search for a number to call. On the other hand, some sites actively encourage you by giving you a discount for booking online.

Availability	If you can be flexible about when you travel you will get a better deal. Choose a site that will search for availability and prices a few days before or after your preferred dates, so giving you more choice over what you pay.
Flexibility	Can you travel from anywhere in the UK and at the drop of a hat? If so, you may be better off using a site that searches all the low-cost airlines rather than going direct to the site of the airline that operates out of a local airport.
	Some sites also let you search for the name of a city rather than an airport code and search all airports rather than specific airports.
Service	Does the site tell you what is included in the price? For example, will you have to pay extra for meals and drinks?
Special needs	Can you pre-book special requirements such as vegetarian meals, bulkhead seats for babies and so on? Does the airline cater for people with a disability?
ATOL information	Will your ticket be protected by ATOL? Some sites give you lots of additional useful information such as travel guides to your destinations, hints and tips on safety, or news on the current situation in a particular country. You may also be interested to know whether the site will email you with its latest offers.

General travel sites

Microsoft's Expedia travel service (*www.expedia.co.uk*) and Travelocity (*www.travelocity.com*) are two travel sites that provide a one-stop shop for flights, holidays, car hire, accommodation, city guides and much more. Travelocity provides access to more than 700 airlines, 55,000 hotels and 50 car rental companies for its members (membership is free). It also has a fare-watcher service that tracks up to five cities of your choice on a daily basis and lets you know as the fares change. Other sites that you can try include Travel Select (*www.travelselect.com*) and Travel4Less (*www.travel4less.co.uk*) both part of lastminute.com, and Ebookers (*www.ebookers.com*) and Cheap flights (*www.cheapflights.co.uk*).

Price-comparison sites

Price-comparison sites (see also Chapter 7) search through several Internet sites for you. Kelkoo (*www.kelkoo.co.uk*), for example, searches Expedia, Opodo and Ebookers, and provides a list of sites that offer competitive prices for airport parking, car hire, ferries, international and national train tickets, and travel insurance. Flight Comparison (*www.flightcomparison.co.uk*) searches Ebookers, Expedia, TravelSelect and Travel4Less.

You might also like to try SkyScanner (*www.skyscanner.net/ wings.asp*). It searches all the major budget airlines and lists the cheapest flights to Europe. The site has a novel look and feel, graphically illustrating all the fares for a given route over a month. You can also search for the three cheapest flights for each day of the month on your chosen route, find the cheapest flights for a specified date and find a weekend break in a European city that comes within your budget.

Consolidators

A number of companies buy seats in bulk to get a discounted rate from the airline, some of which they pass on to you. If you are going to buy through these sites you need to be very clear on the terms and conditions as they can vary considerably from other sites. Major flight consolidators include Travelmood (*www.travelmood.com*), Travelbag (*www.travelbag.co.uk*), Bridge the World (*www.bridgetheworld.com*) and Trailfinders (*www.trailfinders.co.uk*). For a list of other flight consolidators, use a search engine.

Travel auctions

Using travel auctions is not for the faint-hearted, but if you read up on how the sites operate and make sure you know what you are letting yourself in for before you make a bid, you can snap up some real bargains. Different auction sites work in slightly different ways, so it is important to read the help or Frequently

Asked Questions sections of each individual site (see also Chapter 7). Some require you to give your credit-card details before you begin, and take your money as soon as your bid is matched, so beware.

The general idea is that you name the price you are willing to pay for a flight and if the bid is accepted then you will be expected to buy. Here are a few sites for you to try. Priceline (*www.priceline.co.uk*) works with a series of branded partners and boasts that it can save you up to 40 per cent on deals sold to the general public. You tell it what you are looking for, how much you want to pay and the site tries to find it for you. The catch is that you have to be flexible as neither the airline nor the flight times is revealed to you until after you have bought your tickets. You can also try *www.cqout.co.uk*, *www.skyauction.com*, *www.auctions.lastminute.com* and *www.ebay.co.uk*.

Once you have purchased a flight, most tickets are non-changeable/non-refundable. Even if you are able to request a change to a ticket both the airline and the auction site may make a substantial charge, thus negating any benefit you might have gained from netting a cheap ticket in the first place.

Booking online

What is covered?	ALWAYS read the small print. What does your booking cover and what will you have to pay for as extras? For example, check to make sure that there is no delivery charge for tickets or fee for making the booking in the first place. Double-check your booking. During some research carried out by *Holiday Which?* in March 2001, one site miscalculated the price and another misquoted the number of days required.
Credit card	Do you have to pay extra if you pay by credit card?
Cancellation	Is there a cancellation period?
Security	Make sure that you give credit-card details only via a secure site (one that shows a closed padlock or unbroken key usually in the bottom right-hand corner of the screen or https:// in

the address line) and never give details by
email (see Chapter 7). A secure site makes sure
that credit-card and other personal details are
sent in code. You will usually get a message on
the screen to tell you that you are entering a
secure part of the site.

Electronic tickets

Some companies issue electronic tickets rather than the traditional
paper ones. This simply means that the details of your flight are
kept on the airline's computer and all you have to do is check in.
You should, however, be sent a confirmation of your details either
in the post or by email. Make sure that details such as names of
people travelling, dates, times, and so on are correct and that you
take this confirmation along with your passport to the check-in
desk. You may also need to show the credit card that you used to
make the booking.

Worldwide flights

While many of the bargains to be had are for short flights, the
Internet has made it much easier to compare prices among long-
haul operators. And savings on long-haul deals can be proportion-
ately much more rewarding (see case history below). However, if
you have an itinerary that includes multiple destinations it can be
hard to work out costings or routes online. There are a few sites that
are geared up to let you experiment but others will put your
patience to the test. If this proves to be the case, it might be better to
use the Internet to research your destinations and get some idea of
costs before approaching a travel agent to do the hard bit for you.
For example, a travel agent might be able to cut costs quickly by
arranging for you to travel via another European city rather than
taking a direct flight from home to your destination, or recommend
that you purchase a round-the-world ticket rather than a standard
long-haul ticket with a few stopovers.

You could, of course, book tickets on no-frills carriers in other
countries. To find the relevant sites try typing 'budget airlines',
followed by the name of the country you are visiting, into a
search engine.

For your protection

Air Travel Organisers' Licensing (ATOL)

If you book your ticket through a travel agency, by law it must either give you a ticket the minute you pay or provide you with a document confirming that your money is protected by the Civil Aviation Authority's ATOL. ATOL is the only protection scheme for flights or air holidays and is your way of safeguarding your money should the firm go bust, either before you travel or while you are away. Don't confuse this with the Association of British Travel Agents (ABTA), whose protection scheme covers non-air holidays.

Case history

Janine is heading out to Australia for two weeks in October. She is on a mailing list with two flight consolidators, and receives regular updates on special offers. Both companies have a general search facility and she used this to find the cheapest flight for the period when she wanted to travel. Both the sites came up with Singapore Airlines, arriving at the location at the same time but taking a slightly different route. One quoted £647 and the other £1,977.30.

As this was quite a substantial difference Janine decided to try a few flight-comparison sites. One came up with the same Singapore Airlines flight at a price of £862. Another quoted her £630 for the same flight, and the airline itself quoted £800.

The difference between the cheapest quote (£630) and the most expensive quote (£1,977.30) was £1,347.30. Janine considered the hour that it had taken her to do her searches to be time well spent!

Tip

Charter flights are usually covered by ATOL but scheduled flights may not be. If this is the case, your agent may be able to insure against the cost of the ticket should the airline go bust. Otherwise, for purchases over £100 consider paying by credit card as the card company may well reimburse you for any loss.

If you have cause to make a complaint against an airline and subsequently feel that your complaint has not been dealt with fairly, you can approach the Air Transport Users Council (ATUC) (*www.caa.co.uk/auc/default.asp*), the consumer watchdog for the airline industry.

General information on flying

Fear of flying

Are you frightened of flying? There are lots of resources available on the Net to help conquer your fear. Try following this link to an article produced by BUPA, *www.bupa.co.uk/health_information/asp/healthy_living/general/fear_of_flying/*. Many of the major airlines also provide courses (see *www.aviatours.co.uk/*).

Industry news

If you have a particular interest in air safety or industry news, visit the Civil Aviation Authority website (*www.caa.co.uk/*).

UK airports

You can get information about all the major airports around the UK and Ireland from *www.a2bAirports.com*. The site includes information on car parks and gives hotline numbers so that you can enquire about flight schedules. The British Airports Authority (*www.baa.co.uk*) also gives out information about Britain's major airports.

Rail travel

Since the privatisation of British Rail many consumers have been left confused about which train companies run where and who they should contact to get the best price for a journey. This is where the Internet comes to the rescue. There are Internet sites that show you UK rail route maps. You can search for seat availability and prices to match your planned journey and book your ticket online.

National timetables, routes and fares

National Rail Enquiries Online

Typing *www.nationalrail.co.uk/planmyjourney/* in the Address box will take you to National Rail Enquiries Online. This site will give you lots of information, including the latest service disruptions, a directory of train companies, a list of phone numbers for ticket sales, details of rail-cards and current promotions by type or company, and live departure boards for more than 400 stations around the country. The site also provides contact details for disabled passengers who may need assistance at any of the stations on their journey.

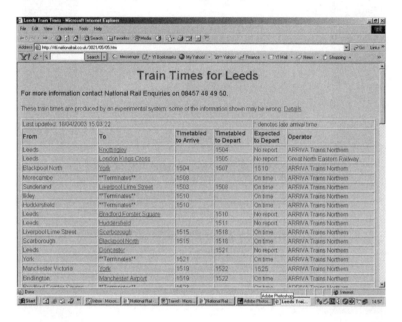

In order to see a timetable, you will need to enter some travel details such as the dates of your outward and return journeys and the approximate departure times from each station.

When you've done that, a timetable will be displayed. You can choose to search for earlier or later trains.

If you have found the information that you want, you can complete the online form with further details such as the number of passengers travelling, the type of fare that you want and so on. The site will then give you an idea of fares and availability for that route.

You can also get links to National Rail timetables at *www. networkrail.co.uk/*.

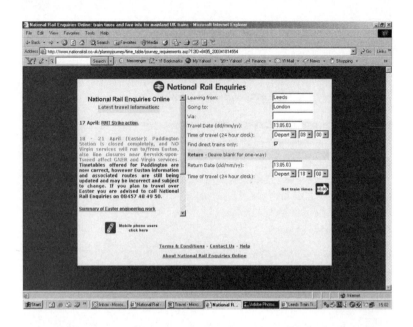

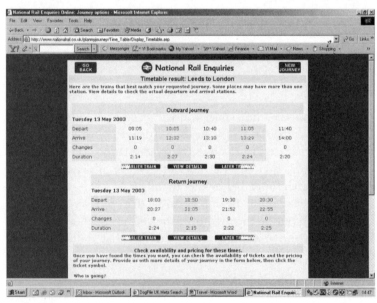

Booking online

There are several general search sites that you can use to find train times and book tickets online. Trainline (*www.thetrainline.com*) will give you up-to-date train timetables for anywhere in mainland UK and find you a ticket to match your requirements (for example, cheapest price or quickest journey). Although the site is produced by Virgin, the results will show you all rail companies for that route. Qjump (*www.qjump.co.uk/index.jsp*) provides a similar service. You plan a journey by entering a start and destination station followed by dates and rough times of travel. Qjump will then produce a list of trains from which you can choose the most convenient. It also shows a list of all the available fares in price order. Both sites are quick and easy to use.

Alternatively, if you know the name of the company that you want to travel with, you can go direct to its site. For example, Great North Eastern Railways (GNER) is at *www.gner.co.uk* and Virgin Trains at *www.virgintrains.co.uk/*.

Case history

Hamid needed to book two tickets from Leeds to London. First of all he used National Rail Enquiries Online to see what companies operated in the Yorkshire region. He then searched for a ticket for the date and times that he wanted to travel. The cheapest option appeared to be £50 return. Not content to accept that the site had found all possible fares, Hamid then searched Qjump and Virgin, both of which came up with the same-priced ticket.

The next day Hamid phoned the National Rail Enquiries line and was told that GNER had a saver ticket for £25 return. 'I was convinced that this meant that the Internet sites had not been able to offer me the best deal. I decided to check the same sites again. I went to the GNER site, Trainline and Qjump, but had to admit that I was wrong. All three sites had up-to-date information and came up with the £25 ticket! Unfortunately there were no seats available at this price but I did manage to get a ticket for £36. And I had the option to reserve a non-smoking window seat. However, I have since spoken to friends who have found a cheaper ticket by phoning than by searching Internet sites so I think I will always be inclined to double-check.'

UK Public Transport Information Service

The UK Public Transport Information Service also produces an excellent site at *www.pti.org.uk/*. It provides information on every aspect of travel within the UK and between the UK and Ireland. It also covers rail, coach and ferry travel between the UK and continental Europe. The site is extremely well laid out and comprehensive, giving you access to timetables, fares, ticket types as well as passenger facilities. The site is not a price-comparison site, but it provides links to other useful sites.

To start off with, try clicking on the area of the country that you live in and choose local rail. You will get to see every type of rail journey that you could go on from your locality. Whatever area of the country you are going to, there are lots of useful sites that you can visit for information. If you select London as your local region, for example, it will provide you with links to city maps via *www.transportforlondon.gov.uk/tfl/*, zone and fare guides to the Underground via a link to *http://tube.tfl.gov.uk*, a guide to the Docklands Light Railway at *www.tfl.gov.uk/dlr/* and timetables for the Heathrow Express at *www.heathrowexpress.com*.

International travel

If you want to travel by rail through Europe, try Railbookers *(www. railbookers.com/.*) It can give you information on individual journeys, tailor-made trips or rail passes for different countries. It can also sort you out with a hire car and restaurant vouchers. Whether you are heading for a European city or somewhere in the UK, this site may prove very useful. It is well laid out, quick and easy to use, and informative.

At *www.eurostar.com* you can find timetables and prices for train journeys to several destinations on the Continent, and book online.

Special trips by rail

If you like rail journeys that are a little out of the ordinary, try keying in the words 'train travel' in a search engine followed by the part of the world you want to go to.

Sea travel

For the independent traveller, going to the Continent has never been easier and, as with the other forms of travel covered in this chapter, numerous Internet sites compete for your attention. This section concentrates on ferry crossings from the UK to Ireland, Scotland and continental Europe. For information on cruises refer to Chapter 9.

Crossings and prices

Crossings from the UK

The quality of ferry-related Internet sites varies tremendously. One of the best sites is the UK Ferry Directory (*www.uk-ferry-directory.co.uk*). It is a one-stop-shop aimed at helping you get all the information you need quickly, easily and at the best price possible. You can use the search facility, follow links to a wide range of ferry-related sites, compare prices for all carriers and routes, find special offers, get a list of websites for all UK ports, and read up on the tips and tricks to make the most of your ferry crossings. The Ferry Information Service site (*www.ferryinformationservice.co.uk/*) is also well worth a visit. It too contains a comprehensive list and links to all ferry companies. It also provides a map showing all routes to Europe as well as tips on driving in each country.

On the other hand, if all you want is to find the cheapest way of getting to your destination, try *www.cheap-ferry-ticket-finder.co.uk/*. The site is easy on the eye and simple to find your way around. It has a cheap-ticket finder which works out the cheapest ferry ticket price for your chosen route. It monitors price changes daily and displays up-to-the-minute promotions.

Other price-comparison sites include *www.directferries.co.uk*, *www.ferries.co.uk*, *www.aferry.to/* and *www.ferrysavers.com*. All four sites are pretty similar and offer prices and information for crossings to most European destinations and the opportunity to book online.

For crossings to islands off the coast of Scotland, try Caledonian MacBrayne (*www.calmac.co.uk*) and Stena (*www.stenaline.co.uk*); for crossings to Ireland visit Irish Ferries (*www.irishferries.ie*), Stena and Ireland Ferries (*www.irelandferry.co.uk*).

Further afield

If you are planning a trip further afield then try using a search engine to search for passenger ferries in the part of the world you are visiting.

Taking your pets

Several sites give you all the information you need to enable you to take your pet with you. The Department for Environment, Food &

Rural Affairs (*www.defra.gov.uk/*) provides information on the PETS travel scheme and quarantine. You could also try Le Dog Stop (*www.ledogstop.com/*) for information on all aspects of pet travel including a rundown of the quarantine process and your options, and pet holiday insurance.

Road travel

Cars

Route planners and maps

Online maps and route planners are likely to change forever the way you plan your journeys.

On the AA route planner (*www.theaa.com/travelwatch/planner_main.jsp*) all you have to do is to select a region, say where you are starting from, where you are going to and what you want to visit *en route*. You can also choose to avoid toll roads, London congestion charging and motorways, or take a route that is suitable for caravans. The route planner will also give you return directions. Your journey will be broken down into small manageable steps, giving you all the information that you need to get you from door to door.

Multimap (*www.multimap.com*) is another high-profile site and has received commendations for the usefulness of its service. You can get street-level maps of the UK, USA and continental Europe as well as road maps of the world and point-to-point travel directions. Multimap also provides a range of supporting services that can help you to find accommodation and restaurants in the locality and book train tickets.

Maporama (*www.maporama.com*) allows you to plan a journey to anywhere in Europe. It provides maps outlining each stage of your journey along with details of the route and other useful information about the area. Interestingly, you can also specify the speed that you are likely to be driving at and it will calculate both the distance and length of the trip. You can even receive your route via email. A few other sites worth a visit include *www.getmethere.co.uk*, *www.map24.co.uk* and *www.viamichelin.com*.

Breakdown organisations

The Internet is a useful place for comparing the services on offer by a range of motoring organisations. Try the AA (*www.theaa.com/*), the

RAC (*www.rac.co.uk*) and Greenflag (*www.greenflag.co.uk*). In addition for European breakdown cover have a look at *www.vehicle-rescue.com/* and *www.internationalbreakdown.com/*.

Stuck in traffic?

Getting struck in traffic can be immensely frustrating, so try to avoid any troublesome spots by visiting the Highways site (*www.highways. gov.uk/*) before you set off on your journey. The site will show you an interactive map of roadworks across England and give details of traffic speed and volume on the M25. If you do get stuck in traffic – and have a laptop computer and a mobile phone – connect to a site called 5 Minutes Away (*www.5minutesaway.co.uk/*). It will give you a list of services within five minutes of any motorway junction in the UK. You can search for the nearest petrol station, accommodation, food and places of interest within three miles of every junction listed. It also gives directions on how to get to each facility and assures the traveller that all listings have car parking nearby.

Car hire

If you want to hire a car your best bet is to start with some price-comparison sites such as *www.expedia.co.uk*, *www.travelocity.com*, *www.holidayautos.co.uk*, *www.ebookers.com* and *www.carhire4less.co.uk*. They all search extensive databases of car-hire companies looking for the best deals. Alternatively, you could go directly to the website of leading car-hire firms such as Hertz (*www.hertz.co.uk*) or Avis (*www.avis.com*) and check out their prices and services before making a comparison.

Although you might expect online car hire to be quite straightforward, there are a few things that you should consider before making an online booking.

- Can you pick up and drop off in different locations?
- Does the site specify a pick-up and drop-off time and, if so, will there be a charge if you drop off late?
- Does the company have locations across the country or just at major airports?
- Are you able to specify type of car, model, size, boot capacity and so on?
- Can you pre-order child seats?
- Does the price include Collision Damage Waiver (CDW)?
- Does the price include unlimited mileage?

As with all online documents, make sure that you read the small print so that you know exactly what you are signing up for.

Coaches or buses

If you want information on local coach or bus services one of the best sites is that of the UK Public Transport Information Service (*www.pti.org.uk*) mentioned above. The A2btravel site (*www.a2btravel.com/bus*) also provides information on timetables and fares for all major coach services across the UK.

On a national level, use the National Express site (*www.nationalexpress.com*). It includes information and online booking facilities for Eurolines (the company's low-cost fares to Europe, *www.eurolines.com*) as well as airport link bus services.

EuroBusExpress also operates an international service connecting major cities in the UK to the Continent. For details see *www.anglia-lines.co.uk/*.

Case history

Catherine, a single mother with two children, recently embarked on the adventure of a lifetime. She drove from the UK to Figline Valdarno in Italy with two children and bikes in tow. She travelled down the Rhine and through Switzerland, stopping at pre-booked campsites and hotels along the way.

'Before we set off I was a little worried about whether I could manage to drive the 3,500 miles without getting lost and without any major catastrophes, given that map reading is not my forte and I hardly speak a word of German! I used the Internet to search for campsites and hotels and booked them all online. Then I used the AA route planner, which gave me every step of the journey in minute detail. It told me how long each leg would take and what kinds of roads I would be travelling on. It even gave me directions to the door of each hotel. I also picked up online guides to some of the major cities that we visited along the way.

'Thankfully, the trip was a resounding success, so much so that we all enthused about taking a year off to travel around the world! The route planning and timings were absolutely perfect and the hotels and campsites were eagerly awaiting our arrival.'

Chapter 9

Holidays

The days of patiently sitting with a travel agent for hours on end are a thing of the past. Instead, you can sit in the comfort of your own home and surf the Net for exciting destinations at your leisure. You can explore specialist holidays, pre-book excursions, buy your foreign currency online, read up on your destination before you go and even arrange for someone to look after your pets while you are away. Sorting your holiday arrangements is an area where the Net really comes into its own.

Strange though it may seem, the main problem with looking for a holiday on the Net is that so much information is out there that it can be difficult to know where to begin. One of the main reasons that there are so many sites, of course, is that everyone has a different idea of what makes a good holiday. Accordingly, this chapter is divided into the following sections:

- holidays in the UK and abroad
- specialist holidays such as those for single parents, singles and the over 50s
- up-to-the-minute news and weather in different parts of the world
- consumer protection
- care for your house and pets while you are away.

Chapter 8 covers travelling by different modes of transport, both within the UK and outside. Some of the information in it may be useful to you when you are reading this chapter.

Holidays in the UK

In April 2003 the British Tourist Authority and the English Tourism Council merged to become VisitBritain, to promote Britain's charms to both a national and international market. The new organisation's website (*www.visitbritain.co.uk*) will give you lots of ideas for holidays within the UK, as well as a list of events, attractions and regional tourist offices. There is even a section entitled *Britain for less* that gives details of things that you can do and see for free.

Information Britain (*www.information-britain.co.uk/*) is also well worth a visit. A one-stop shop, it gives information on Britain by area, county and town, and ideas of where you can visit, eat and stay. The site also has lots of useful features such as a daily update on the UK weather, details of tourist information centres throughout the UK, ferries, theatre tickets and even an online euros to pounds currency converter. About Britain (*www.aboutbritain.com*) is an excellent source of information on regional attractions. To make it easy for you to find something to your taste, attractions are grouped into categories such as historic houses, museums, castles and forts, and landmarks and monuments. You can also read up on a town of your choice and come away armed with interesting facts about its industrial heritage, parks and gardens, and nearby towns. For a useful UK travel portal with links to major UK travel-related sites try *www.closerangebritain.com*. The BBC web guide to travel sites around the UK and worldwide, found at *www.bbc.co.uk/webguide/holiday/*, is also well worth a visit.

If you find places of historic interest and outstanding natural beauty interesting, try the National Trust site (*www.nationaltrust.org.uk/main/*). It also does a wonderful version for children at *www.nationaltrust.org.uk/trusty/index_flash.htm*, which includes a list of events taking place around the country. The Walking Britain site (*www.walkingbritain.co.uk*) has over 3,000 pages of information featuring walks in national parks, villages, bridges, mines and churches.

Holidays in the UK are often synonymous with trips to the seaside. The Marine Conservation Society has produced an invaluable guide to British beaches at *www.goodbeachguide.co.uk*, listing those beaches that meet their standards of safety and hygiene.

Holidays abroad

The sky is the limit when it comes to choosing your holiday abroad. Whether you fancy a package holiday in the sun or a once-in-a-lifetime trip to the Antarctic the Internet is the ideal place to make it happen.

Where to start?

If you have never booked a holiday online before it might be best to start off by visiting a range of different sites and see what they have to offer. Look out for sites that provide you with useful information about the destination in which you are interested or anticipate the questions you might have regarding your travel arrangements. Check whether you are able to book online, pre-book excursions or order currency. Do you have the option to choose a tailor-made itinerary or are you being sold a fairly standard package? Is there a telephone number that you can call to get personal assistance before or following an online booking? Investing a little time upfront to explore a range of sites should pay dividends in the long run. You will soon get a feel for those that are best able to meet your needs and those which you should ultimately steer clear of.

Sites

You can opt to book through an online travel agent, tour operator or a company specialising in a particular type of holiday, such as cruises. You can head for a one-stop-shop site (an online holiday shop that provides a whole host of options including package holidays, cars, flights, accommodation, insurance, visa information and travel guides). Or you can look for last-minute bargains. Here are some sites that you can try out. The list is not exhaustive, and the distinction between travel agents, tour operators and one-stop shops is sometimes blurred. You can find more sites by typing keywords into a search engine or by picking up ideas from online magazines such as *Holiday Which?*, which you can access if you are a subscriber to Which? Online.

Travel agents

Company name	Website
Thomas Cook	*www.thomascook.com*
A2btravel	*www.a2btravel.com*
Virgin Holidays	*www.virgin.com*
My Travel	*www.mytravel.com*
eDreams	*www.edreams.com*
Lunn Poly	*www.lunnpoly.com*
Trailfinders	*www.trailfinders.co.uk*
Advantage Travel Centres	*www.advantage4travel.com*

Holiday companies and tour operators

Company name	Website
Thomson Holidays	*www.thomson-holidays.com/*
First Choice	*www.firstchoice.co.uk/*
Airtours	*www.airtours.com*

One-stop shops

Company name	Website
Opodo	*www.opodo.co.uk*
Expedia	*www.expedia.co.uk*

Travelocity	*www.travelocity.com*
Bargain Holidays	*www.bargainholidays.com*
Virgin Travel Store	*www.virgintravelstore.com*
Cheap Flights	*www.cheapflights.co.uk*

Specialist companies

Although the majority of people on package holidays opt for a beach holiday in the sun, some choose an activity holiday such as skiing, water sports or cycling. Substantial numbers of people also go on cruises each year and many couples get married in exotic locations abroad. So if you want to do something slightly out of the ordinary, using a search engine to search for a specialist area is a good way to go. Here are a few useful sites in some categories.

Golf

Golf Breaks	*www.golfbreaks.com*
Great Golf Holidays	*www.greatgolfholidays.com/*
Long Shot Golf	*www.longshotgolf.co.uk/*

Skiing

Ski Holidays	*www.ski-holidays.com*
Ski Club of Great Britain	*www.skiclub.co.uk*
Ski and Snowboard Directory	*www.ski.co.uk*

Cycling

| Country Lanes | *http://dspace.dial.pipex.com/countrylanes/* |
| Wide Open Road | *www.wideopenroad.co.uk/* |

Adventure

Discover the World	*www.discover-the-world.co.uk*
Travelbag Adventures	*www.travelbag-adventures.com*
If You Explore	*www.ifyouexplore.com/*
Campfire	*www.campfire.co.uk/*

Cruises

Cruise Line	*www.cruiseline.co.uk*
Cruise Direct	*www.worldcruisedirect.com*
Why Not Cruise	*www.whynotcruise.co.uk/*

If you can afford to be flexible and take a last-minute holiday then try *www.lastminute.com*, *www.latedeals.co.uk*, *www.bargainholidays.com* and *www.go-nowtravel.com*. However, it is always worth taking a few minutes to compare prices with those found on other sites just to make sure that your last-minute holiday is the bargain you think it is. Late deals also often require you to book over the phone rather than online.

Accommodation

For the independent traveller, finding accommodation in the right location and at the right price can make all the difference to a holiday. You can either head straight for the site of a reputable hotel chain such as *www.marriott.com*, *www.holiday-inn.com* or *www.bestwestern.com*, or visit a site that will give you a listing of hotel chains and search the one of your choice, such as All Hotel Chains (*www.all-hotel-chains.com/hotel-chain/hotel-chain-directory.htm*) or Rooms Plus (*www.roomsplus.com/chains/looks*). If you want to try out a directory website visit www.accommodation.com or *www.hotelregister.com*. For B&Bs, try *www.beduk.co.uk*.

Alternatively, you can use a one-stop travel site such as Travelocity (*www.travelocity.com*) or general accommodation sites such as *www.placestostay.com*, *www.travelselect.com* or *www.travelcare.co.uk*. They will search a number of different hotels to find the best rate for you.

As with other forms of travel, it is always best to check a few sites to make sure that you have a good deal. Prices can vary from agency to agency depending upon the kinds of deals that they have negotiated with the hotel. Some buy rooms in bulk so that they can get a discounted rate, others approach a hotel on your behalf and take commission and still others try to sell rooms that would otherwise remain empty. In a *Which?* survey carried out in September 2002, there was a tremendous discrepancy in prices quoted by agencies for the same accommodation. For rooms in a hotel in Amsterdam agencies quoted up to £64 less than booking with the hotel direct and for three nights in a hotel in Boston one agency quoted £261 less than the hotel. However, the reverse was also true. Sometimes the agency prices were higher than booking direct. It will, therefore, pay you to shop around a little and at least to check out the price being quoted by the hotel itself.

And again, if you are able to go last minute, check out *www.wotif.com*, *www.lastminute.com* and *www.laterooms.co.uk*.

> **Tip**
>
> If you have your heart set on a particular hotel, don't give up at the first hurdle. You might find availability through one site but not another.
>
> Don't search according to star rating or price as you might find a cheaper room available at a hotel with a higher star rating.

Currency

Some holiday sites offer you the option to book your currency online. Otherwise you can order via sites such as Thomas Cook (*www.thomascook.com*), Royal Mail travel services (*www.royalmail.com*) or OnlineFX (*www.onlinefx.co.uk*). Typically you will be able to buy notes or travellers cheques in different currencies and have them delivered next day to the address on your credit card. However, conditions of sale may vary between sites so it is important to read the help or Frequently Asked Questions sections of each site. For instance, Thomas Cook places an upper ceiling value of £1,500 on each order and gives you the option to pick up your currency from one of its local branches. A good site should also email you with confirmation of the order.

You can use a currency converter to check that you are getting a good deal. Try *www.xe.com/ucc* or *http://finance.yahoo.com/m3?u*.

Once you have decided on your destination you could print out a list of Automated Teller Machines (ATMs) for the region that you are visiting. If you want a list of ATMs that will take your Visa credit card go to *http://international.visa.com/ps/services/atmnetwork.jsp*. If you have a MasterCard/Maestro/Cirrus card, then *www.mastercard.com/cardholderservices/atm/* will give you a list of cash machines worldwide.

Virtual tours

One of the major advantages of using the Internet to find that perfect holiday has to be the fact that some sites allow you to 'travel' around places of interest, take a tour inside your accommodation or look at live webcam links and all without leaving your PC. The Internet has made virtual travel a reality. Admittedly, the number of sites that currently offer these facilities are few and far between, but it is more than likely that as technology improves and Internet access speeds increase, more and more sites will use these methods to entice you to buy.

The Armchair Travel Company Ltd (*www.armchair-travel.com*), for example, offers a virtual tour of Kew Gardens and the Taj Mahal. If you are thinking of renting a holiday cottage, why not take a look inside each room before you make your decision? Visit *www.cottages4you.co.uk*, choose the area you want to visit and click on 'Virtual tours' when you find a cottage that meets your needs. You can also get a virtual guide around London at *www. a-london-guide.co.uk*, scenic views across England from the BBC at *www.bbc.co.uk/england/webcams/tour/* and live views of San Francisco at *www.mapwest.com*.

Specialist holidays

Children

Keeping children occupied during the school holidays can be a real challenge. The Net is a useful source of specialist holiday groups that cater for children and their many needs. This section concentrates on children's activity groups and camps (see Chapter 8 for information on family holidays).

If you want a comprehensive list of just what's out there, start with a directory site such as the UK Children's Directory (*www. ukchildrensdirectory.com/*). If you click on 'Activities' you can then choose from a range of categories such as the arts, camps and holidays and travel. Each category will provide you with information on groups that tailor special holiday packages for children. You might also like to try Summer Fun for Kids (*www.summerfun4kids.co.uk*). The site is nicely laid out and easy to find your way around, with good descriptions of registered sites that provide day courses and camps for children. Unfortunately, at the time of writing, only a small number of registered sites were on the list, but it is worth re-visiting the site from time to time to see if the list has grown.

To be on the safe side
Safety is by far the most important issue on most parents' minds when they consider any kind of independent adventure holiday for

their children. Two websites are a must for any safety-conscious parents. One is the Adventure Activities Licensing Authority site (*www.aala.org.uk/*). The AALA carries out inspections of activity-centre providers on behalf of the Department of Education and Skills (DfES) and issues a licence to those that meet the national standard of good practice. You can use the site to search for licence holders. Equally as important, the British Activity Holiday Association (BAHA, *www.baha.org.uk/*), is the trade association for private companies providing activity holidays. Members of the association have agreed to adhere to the BAHA code of practice (a copy of which can be read online), standards of staff training and accommodation. BAHA also publishes a consumer guide to help those who are looking for an activity holiday at home or abroad.

Before you decide which company to choose, check out the website thoroughly. Read the 'About us' and Frequently Asked Questions sections and make sure that you are satisfied that the company will provide a safe and secure environment for your child. This checklist may help.

Things to consider	Questions
Owners	Who owns the company?
Established	How long has it been operating?
Safety record	What is its safety record like? Have there ever been any serious accidents?
Accreditations	Is it endorsed by other reputable organisations?
Qualifications	What qualifications do staff have?
Recruitment	How does it recruit and vet staff?
Policies	What are its policies on bullying, accidents and so on?

General holidays and camps

If you have a child who is a budding popstar, wizard or circus performer, or one who would like to try his or her hand at becoming a secret agent, Indiana Jones or learner driver, check out PGL Adventure holidays (*www.pgl.co.uk/online/*). These activities are only a taster of those on offer – PGL offers an extensive list of activities both here and abroad, sure to appeal to children of all ages and interests. It is a member of the BAHA and complies with safety regulations imposed by the AALA. The site gives full details of staff qualifications and training.

Camp Beaumont (*www.campbeaumont.com/*) also offers a wide range of interesting-sounding pastimes for the summer vacation. It has seven non-residential camps around London, and four residential ones in England. Children attend for a minimum of a week, and have a range of activities to choose from each day.

If sporting activities are your child's thing then you are pretty much spoilt for choice. Try Kings Sports Camps (*www.kingssportscamps. com/*). The organisation has 300 camps operating from 60 venues across the UK. The camps are not residential and children can attend on a daily basis in weekly blocks. You may also like to try Barracudas (*www.barracudas.co.uk*), which provides activity camps for children aged 5–14 years that include motor sports, archery, drama as well as basic sports such as swimming. Adventure and Computer Holidays (*www.holiday-adventure.co.uk/*) provides both day camps and residential holidays. Run by qualified teachers, instructors and activity specialists, it aims to give children a fun and educational experience. It is also accredited by BAHA and claims to hold a faultless Ofsted inspection record.

In addition to providing a range of activities to suit all tastes, some companies allow children the opportunity to focus on particular skills. For example, Supercamps (*www.supercamps.co.uk/academies.htm*) runs sports, drama and art academies.

Music holidays
Music holidays (*www.musicale.co.uk/music-holidays.html*) offers non-residential courses at 18 venues across England, for children of all abilities in the 5–16 age bracket. It also runs a residential course in Harpenden for advanced players up to the age of 18.

Sick, disabled and disadvantaged children
There are many sites dedicated to taking care of the needs of sick, disabled and underprivileged children. Some are general sites that cater for children with a range of disabilities, such as Dave Lee's Happy Holidays (*www.davelee.org.uk*), a charity providing holidays for disabled, sick and underprivileged children of Kent and their families. The National Holiday Fund (*www.nhfcharity.co.uk/*) has taken 300 severely ill or disabled children on holiday to Disney World in Florida since it first began in 1987. Some, like Break (*www.break-charity.org*), aim to give families of children with special

needs a rest. Others, such as the Harvest Trust (*www.users.dircon. co.uk/~hartrust/*), provide holidays for underprivileged children.

If you are caring for someone with a specific disability who may require special holiday arrangements, use a search engine to search for the name of the disability +holidays. Examples of charities helping children with specific conditions include Dream Holidays Charity (*www.cfdreamholidays.com/*), which helps families with children who have Cystic Fibrosis, and Sense (*www.sense.org.uk/ holidays/*), which organises summer holidays for around 120 deaf and blind children, ranging from abseiling in the Isle of Wight to white-water rafting in Wales.

Teenagers and young adults

The teenage years present their own challenges for parents trying to strike the right balance between independence and parental responsibility. Many travel companies provide clubs where teenagers can spread their wings a little while still remaining within the confines of the family holiday. However, for something a little bit more adventurous, try Outposts holidays (*www.outposts.co.uk/outposts/ holidays/holidaysfront.htm*). It organises family and group holidays on location in South Africa. The holidays take in the history, ecology and wildlife of the region as well as providing a range of adventure activities.

The British Universities North America Club (BUNACAMP) allows people aged between 19 and 35 the opportunity to work with children, mainly teaching sports in summer camps throughout the USA. You can find more details on its site (*www.bunac.org*).

Holidays for the over 50s

Many people over 50 have more time and money to spend on international travel than ever before and, as a result, a number of dedicated sites have emerged in recent years.

Many of these sites act as portals (one-stop shops) covering a whole range of services, of which travel is just one. But although they are not dedicated holiday sites, the travel options they present are made with the particular age group in mind. For an introduction to these sites, have a look at *www.over50s.com/, www.50connect. co.uk/, www.cennet.co.uk/* and *www.silversurfers.net/*. Silver Surfers, for example, regularly monitors the Net on the look-out for sites that its audience will appreciate, and its holiday offerings cover everything from action holidays to gentle strolls around the English countryside.

The SAGA group is already well known for the excellent services provided for people in this age group. Its travel website (*www.saga.co.uk/travel*) caters for a very wide range of tastes and budgets, and provides advice on travelling, insurance cover and destinations. You can even book your foreign currency online through the site.

If you are after a specific type of holiday, look out for the 'seniors' sections on travel sites or search for the particular activity in which you are interested. For example, Explore Holidays (*www.exploreholidays.com/*) caters for walking holidays for the over 50s in the Canadian Rockies. Skiers would find *www.fiftyplusnorthantsadventureclub.org.uk/othersites.htm* useful. The site invites you to check out the eccentric 'Over The Hill Gang' (*www.skiersover50.com*) who run 30 trips a year for skiers of a certain age.

Holidays for disabled people

If you suffer from a disability, have a look at the Disabled Holiday Directory (*www.disabledholidaydirectory.co.uk*). It has links to holiday accommodation and services for disabled people in the UK, Ireland, continental Europe and the USA, and gives full details of disabled facilities for each of the properties listed.

Holiday Care (*www.holidaycare.org.uk*) provides information about transport, accommodation, visitor attractions, activity holidays and respite-care establishments, both in the UK and overseas, which enables people with all kinds of disability to holiday where possible in a mainstream environment.

Another useful site is Abletogo.Com (*www.abletogo.com*). To use it, you will need to register your details on the site but membership is free. You can carry out a basic search for different types of accommodation in an area or an advanced search that will help to find accommodation suitable for your personal needs. Youreable.com (*www.youreable. com*) offers more than just travel information, but on the travel front you can browse accommodation in the UK, attractions, holidays abroad, specialised holidays and get information on travel agents, a Disabled Persons Railcard or hiring holiday equipment.

For an excellent choice of holidays and tours for all, try Can Be Done at *www.canbedone.co.uk/*, Access Travel (*www.access-travel.co.uk/*) and Accessible Travel (*www.accessibletravel.co.uk/*). For accommodation in the UK try *www.like2stay.co.uk/*.

A couple of sites make excellent reading for the disabled traveller. For general ideas and information try *www.disabilityview.co.uk/ holidays.shtml*. If you are considering booking a Virgin holiday then read *www.virginholidays.co.uk/cities/vitalinfo/specialneeds.shtml*.

Singles

Whatever your reasons for contemplating a singles holiday there are plenty of sites that are dedicated to helping you achieve just that. Of course, singles holidays can be a sensitive issue for many people, and getting the right package will be half the battle. For example, some sites stress that they are not a dating agency, while others dangle the romance angle as a carrot. If you want to see exactly what's out there, start by visiting a directory of singles holidays like *www.travel-quest.co.uk/tqsingles.htm*. The following sites will give you an indication of what's on offer and inspire you to search for something that will suit your personal circumstances.

Solo's Holidays (*www.solosholidays.co.uk/content/index.asp*) claims to be the UK's number one tour operator for single people. Holidays are organised according to age, and each group is accompanied by a tour manager. Solitair holidays (*www.solitairhols.co.uk/holidays.html*) provides an assortment of holidays in Europe, Asia, Africa and the Caribbean. It offers party weekend events, short breaks that allow you to sample the experience before you take the plunge of a holiday away. Once on holiday you can choose to do things as part of a group or go off and do your own thing.

Friendship Travel (*www.friendshiptravel.com/*) provides an assortment of holidays for the single traveller, including cruises and skiing packages. Club Individual (*www.clubindividual.gr/*) also organises holidays in Crete that are sensitively tailored to the needs of the single traveller.

Holidays for single-parent families

For single-parent families taking time out to relax on holiday together can be an important part of the social calendar, but it can also be a time that many dread. Will there be other single-parent families around? How will you occupy your evenings when the children have gone to bed? If you would appreciate a group holiday with other single-parent families check out Small Families (*www.smallfamilies.co.uk*) and One Parent Family Holidays (*http://members.aol.com/opfholiday/*). The latter has been operating since 1975 and its holidays for 2004 include a round-the-world tour taking in South Africa, Australia, New Zealand, the Pacific and America.

For an excellent source of information and inspiration try *www.singleparents.about.com/cs/holidays/*. Although the site is American, there are lots of interesting articles including surviving holidays spent without your children and handling holidays as a single parent.

News, weather and travel

Foreign and Commonwealth Office

If you are travelling to a destination that is under threat of war, terrorist attack, political upheaval, or is involved in a major health scare, then visiting the Foreign and Commonwealth Office site (*www.fco. gov.uk*) is a must. The site provides lots of information to help keep British travellers safe while abroad. You can select links to particular countries and get advice both on how to prepare for your trip as well as what you can do if things go wrong. The site is kept up to date throughout the day with the latest press releases, ministerial speeches and statements.

News agencies

The BBC's coverage of international news and weather is unrivalled. You can find all of the services through the home page (*www.bbc.co.uk*), or you can go direct to the weather page by typing *www.bbc.co.uk/weather/*. You can get a five-day weather forecast for any place in the UK by typing in the postcode or picking a city from the drop-down list. If you are heading off to continental Europe you can get a forecast, and the country guides give you information on climates around the world. The site offers an impressive 5,000 worldwide weather forecasts.

Of course the BBC is not the only news agency to provide travel news and weather forecasts, and there are also many dedicated weather sites to boot. For travel try CNN (*www.cnn.com/travel/*) and for CNN weather try *www.cnn.com/weather*.

If you take more than a passing interest in the weather, you might be better off going to a dedicated site that will give you comprehensive coverage. Try *www.accuweather.com* or *www. Intellicast.com*. The Met Office site (*www.metoffice.gov.uk/*) provides weather reports and warnings for the UK and continental Europe.

Online newspapers

Most British newspapers have an online presence, so you can keep in touch even when you are travelling abroad. For example, the online version of *The Times* (*www.timesonline.co.uk*) provides all the latest news. In addition, its travel section has all sorts of fascinating articles such as up-to-date information on health scares, top worldwide destinations, overseas property and hidden treasures. The travel section of *The Guardian* (*http://travel.guardian.co.uk*) is another useful resource.

Travel guides

The Internet will provide you with a wealth of information on almost any holiday destination that you care to think about. You can read up on a region, a city, activities, attractions and much more besides. You will find travel guides available through lots of sites. Here are a few to try out.

www.worldtravelguide.net	This site provides guides to travelling around the world.
www.lonelyplanet.com	Lonely Planet offers comprehensive information on worldwide destinations, telling you the best times to go, what you will find off the beaten track, how to get there and once there, how to get around.
www.frommers.com/	In addition to the usual, Frommers provides a layout of each city as well as useful information such as the number for the consulates, emergency telephone numbers, bank opening times, list of doctors and places that provide Internet access.
www.letsgo.com/	These guides are aimed more at students and give practical information as well as an overview of nightlife, entertainment and festivals.
www.travel.roughguides.com/	This site provides online content for thousands of destinations worldwide.

Consumer protection

Bonds

Before you book a holiday online make sure that the site carries the appropriate logos. For flight or air holidays look for the ATOL sign (see Chapter 8 for more information). For all other types of holidays the agent should be registered with the Association of British Travel Agents (ABTA) or the Association of Independent Tour Operators (AITO). By law, if you are booking a package holiday, the travel company is required to subscribe to a scheme that will recompense you in the event of the company going out of business. ABTA and AITO hold bonds which will pay out if the company goes bust before you get or finish your holiday.

AITO (*www.aito.co.uk/home/index.html*) represents around 160 of the UK's specialist tour operators. The aim of the group is to provide a high level of customer satisfaction through choice, quality and service, so if a company displays the AITO logo then, in theory, you should be on to a winner as far as standards go. As the association represents independent companies, most of which are privately owned, they will generally have a personal vested interest in making sure that customers come back to them. They may also demonstrate a level of expertise that is hard to find in a larger non-specialist travel agent. Most importantly, however, in compliance with UK and European regulations, companies that belong to AITO are vetted and fully bonded. They also agree to abide by AITO's code of business practice, which involves issuing clear and accurate descriptions of holidays and evaluating customer feedback.

Consumer angle

If you have access to Which? Online, consult *Holiday Which?* for information on your rights with respect to holidays and travelling. The Consumer Gateway (*www.consumer.gov.uk/consumer_web/holiday_faq. htm*) is an excellent one-stop consumer shop run by the Department of Trade and Industry (DTI). Apart from all the other consumer information on the site, it is an excellent source of information relating to travel and holidays. It gives you a rundown of the roles of each of the major bodies associated with travel, tells you where to find more information on a range of issues and how to go about making a complaint. There is also a Frequently Asked Questions section that gives answers to the kinds of questions that most of us might ask, such as 'What are my rights if a tour operator is not covered by ABTA/ATOL?' The Citizens Advice Bureau (*www.adviceguide.org.uk*) also has lots of useful advice for travellers.

While you are away

House-sitting

If you would like to get away more often but want the peace of mind of knowing that your house and pets are being looked after, then Homesitters (*www.homesitters.co.uk/*) claims to have just the answer. Its slogan is 'We stay when you're away.' The fact that someone is living in your home means that you can avoid all those nasty winter surprises such as burst pipes and damp. They will look after your pets, do routine home and garden maintenance, water plants, take telephone messages and so on. The site is well produced and answers most of the questions that you would have about having someone you don't know staying in your home. It explains that all sitters are responsible people over the age of 40, employees of the company and undergo a rigorous selection and checking process. Sitters are matched to owners according to your needs. For example, some sitters will be able to take care of horses, others will be dog-lovers and so on. A similar service is provided by Home and Pets (*www.home-and-pets.co.uk/*) and UK Pet Sitters (*www.ukpetsitter.co.uk*).

If you are not particularly keen to have a stranger stay in your home but are still worried about leaving your pets behind when you go away, Pet Chums (*www.petchums.co.uk*) might provide the compromise that you are looking for. It is a London-based company and a member of the National Association of Registered Dogsitters and Pet Sitters International. Its members will feed, walk, clean and play with your pets. They will also open and close curtains, put lights on, pick up newspapers and post, water plants and put some milk in the fridge for your return.

Chapter 10

Buying, selling and moving house

The Internet has revolutionised the property market. Whether you are buying, selling, renting, or looking to build or restore a property, the information and advice you need is at your fingertips. This chapter looks at a number of ways in which the Internet can help you take the stresses out of property deals and remove some of the headaches of home moves.

General websites

For an introduction to a one-stop property site, take a look at a portal site such as House Web (*www.houseweb.co.uk*). It offers a full range of services for the house and home, including selling, buying and renting services, a discussion forum as well as a quoting facility for services such as removals, mortgages and home insurance. House Web estimates that it receives more than 1.2 million visits each year. Another good portal site is *www.reallymoving.com*. This site is particularly good for tips and advice for planning the move.

For an excellent directory-style site, try *www.uk-property-sale-directory.co.uk*. This has collected all the best property sites on the Internet under one roof. You can link to sites specialising in selling properties or those providing information on related areas such as mortgages and conveyancing. There are also links to sites that provide practical advice on moving home.

Buying a property online

The Internet is very useful if you are buying a house, particularly if you are moving to a new location and are unfamiliar with the area.

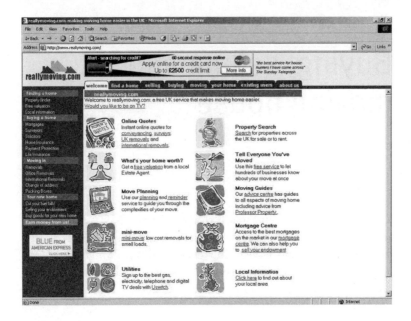

Traditionally, buying a property involves weekend trips around all the local estate agents seeking information. The Internet has made it easier for people to obtain details of property, thereby saving time and a lot of energy.

A new location

If you are moving to a part of the country that is new to you (or even a different part of the city you currently live in), you will need to find a residential area that meets all your needs. You may need to consider schools, routes to work and general amenities. Without personal recommendation it can be difficult to know where exactly to house-hunt. Although the Internet will not have all the answers it will allow you to narrow down the options by investigating the possible residential areas online.

The Up My Street website (*www.upmystreet.com*) is designed specifically for this purpose. All you need to do is enter a postcode and the site will provide a map as well as information on a whole range of amenities including schools, childcare and public transport. You can also find out about property prices in the area as well as the availability of broadband, an important consideration for people with an elife. For further information on the area, take a look at the BBC website (*www.bbc.co.uk*). By typing the postcode into the 'Where I live' box, you will be provided with a link to the local BBCi website which should provide plenty of information on the region.

The Streetmap website (*www.streetmap.co.uk*) is also useful for house-hunting. Simply type in the street name or the postcode for the property you are considering and it will display a detailed map that can be printed. Multimap (*www.multimap.com*) is another help-ful site for finding your way around the UK and abroad. You can locate an area and then zoom in as many times as necessary to view a more detailed map of the area. If you use one of these sites before setting out you should be able to find your way around easily.

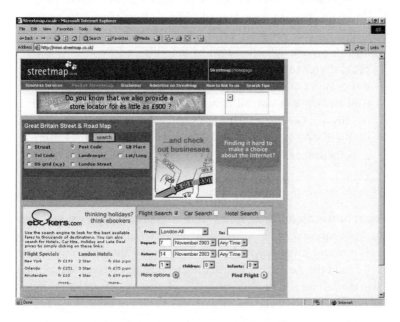

Finding a property

Numerous property websites exist on the Net, with some proving more reliable than others. Look for agents that belong to the Ombudsman for Estate Agents (OEA) or the National Association of Estate Agents (NAEA), as they offer more consumer protection that those that do not.

It is important to receive a detailed account of the property no matter how far you are moving. Ideally this will include pho-

---

Case history

Ruth, a single mum with two young daughters, was finding it hard to make ends meet in London. She had been offered a transfer to a government department in York and was excited by the prospect.

'Not knowing York at all I really didn't know where to start house-hunting. I spent some time looking at the Up My Street website. I have a good friend in York and I typed in her postcode and looked at the area she lives in but quickly discounted it because the house prices were too expensive for me. I also looked up the postcodes of some of the properties I had been sent details of. I was just about to take a couple of days off to travel up there to look around when I came across the site's Conversations option. I wrote a couple of paragraphs about myself, my lifestyle, the ages of the girls and the maximum I could stretch to price-wise. Within a couple of days I had received three replies, all from mums with children of a similar age to my two. Believe it or not, all three recommended the same area of the city and two even named the same primary school! I'm going up there next weekend and will certainly head straight for the area they recommended.'

---

tographs from a number of viewpoints or, preferably, a video showing both internal and external views. This feature is known as a virtual tour and it usually includes a 360-degree shot of a number of rooms and the gardens. This exciting technology has revolutionised both the selling and buying process, and a growing number of estate agents and property sites use it as a major form of marketing. For an example of a site that has successfully incorporated the use of virtual tours take a look at the Scottish property site *www.s1homes.com*.

However, do bear in mind that virtual tours and photographs are likely to exaggerate the strengths of a property while at the same time underestimating or even completely omitting its weaknesses.

Traditional estate agents

It is advisable to make your first port of call the websites of the 'bricks and mortar' estate agents in the area you are moving to.

These will undoubtedly have the largest choice of properties. For a list of local estate agents try *www.yell.co.uk*, the online version of *Yellow Pages* and search for estate agents in the town you are moving to. The entries will include direct links to those estate agents with their own websites.

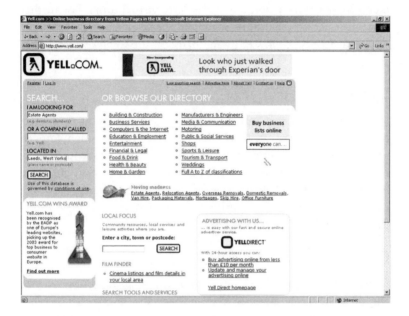

Online property agents

If you do not find a suitable property through the traditional route the next step is to try those agents that have only an online presence. These sites usually have national coverage, and the number of properties available tends to depend on where you are looking. If you are moving to London or one of the larger UK cities you could be spoilt for choice, but if you are looking for a property in a smaller town you may be disappointed. You will also find that some sites simply contain the properties on offer from a range of the traditional estate agencies with very few independent offerings.

Probably the best-known property site is Fish4Homes (*www. fish4homes.co.uk*). This site provides details of properties for sale UK-wide as well as new property developments and a directory of estate agents. It also sends emails to you should a suitable property become available. Other sites with a good national coverage are

Property Finder (*www.propertyfinder.co.uk*) and the Right Move (*www.rightmove.co.uk*). If you are searching for a home on a new development, try *www.smartnewhomes.com*. You can search by region or by developer.

Most of the property details within these sites include photographs and floor plans, and some have virtual tours. For further sites, use a search engine and search on the words 'property for sale' or 'estate agents', followed by the name of the town or region you are looking in.

Sorting out the mortgage

It is advisable to sort out your mortgage before you even start house-hunting. You can then calculate exactly how much you can spend and restrict yourself to looking at properties within your budget. Charcol Online (*www.charcolonline.co.uk*) is just one of the many sites that provide a range of independent financial services including mortgages. For further information on securing a mortgage online, see Chapter 12.

Conveyancing

Conveyancing is the legal and administrative process necessary to complete the sale and/or purchase of a property. Traditionally, a solicitor or licensed conveyancer carries out this service, although you can do it yourself if you live in England or Wales, especially if you are buying a house rather than a flat. Whether you do it yourself or pay an expert there are certain legalities that you have to adhere to when purchasing a property and the process can become very involved. Because of this, some mortgage lenders insist that you employ an expert for the purchasing side of your property move.

Tip

The Scottish system does not lend itself to the DIY approach as solicitors act as estate agents as well as providing conveyancing services. In Northern Ireland there is no reason why you cannot market your own house but the land laws are complex and you will need expert help with the conveyancing.

Easier2move (*www.easier2move.co.uk*) is a site specialising in online conveyancing. It claims to find you a conveyancing solicitor for a guaranteed fixed price, with no hidden extras, on a no-sale (or purchase), no-fee basis. You can follow the progress of your conveyancing online 24 hours a day and you will be kept up to date by email or text message to your mobile phone. Alternatively, try Solicitors Online (*www.solicitors-online.com*). This is the Law Society's website, designed to help you find a residential conveyancing solicitor in England or Wales. If you are purchasing property in Scotland or Northern Ireland try the Law Society of Scotland (*www.lawscot.org.uk*) or the Law Society of Northern Ireland (*www.lawsoc-ni.org*).

Surveys

There is a popular misconception that the bank or building society lending you the money to purchase a property will carry out a full structural survey. In fact, the lender will usually only provide a valuation survey confirming that the property is good security against the mortgage, although it may provide a brief description of any problems that could seriously affect the value of the property.

To find a qualified surveyor in your area access the Royal Institute of Chartered Surveyors' (RICS) website (*http://dir.rics.org*). This will take you to the directory page where you can search for an expert based on your requirements. Alternatively, try Surveyors and Valuers Accreditation (*www.sava.org.uk*). SAVA is an independent standard-setting body for property practitioners who are members of RICS.

Selling a property online

Whether you sell your property yourself or use the services of a traditional estate agent you are likely to find that the Internet will play a part. The majority of estate agents have realised the power of the Internet as a marketing tool and will use it to complement the more standard methods for selling a property such as mailing details to their current database, newspaper advertisements and shop-front displays.

If you decide to sell through a traditional estate agent make sure that it uses the Internet to sell your property because websites run by traditional estate agencies receive thousands of viewers every day.

Pricing your property

If you want to cut out the estate agency and sell your property your-self, the first thing you will need to do is to work out a realistic ask-ing price. Websites such as *www.proviser.com* and *www.hometrack.co.uk* will help you find the average house prices in England and Wales based on area, size and type of property. Alternatively, sites such as Partake (*www.partake.co.uk*) will organise for three estate agents to view and value your property. This service is free of charge and without obligation.

Advertising online

If you decide to go it alone you need to give your property maxi-mum exposure. It is wise to advertise your property through a number of media – a board outside your house, adverts in local and property papers and, of course, the Internet.

Tip

The popular *Daltons Weekly* will automatically place your advert on its website (*www.daltons.co.uk*) free of charge when you place an advert in the magazine, thus providing double exposure. If you place an advert with any paper or magazine it is certainly worth checking whether the ad can also be included on its website.

Many of the larger, national sites do not provide an option for individuals selling their own property. Instead, they guide you to participating estate agents in your area. If you definitely want to go it alone, there are over 100 private-sale sites offering text-only adver-tisements (often for free) or a more comprehensive service at a cost. Housenet (*www.housenet.co.uk*) is one of the longest established web-sites allowing people to advertise their homes for sale. Advert pack-ages start at around £50, significantly cheaper than some competitive sites. The Little House Company (*www.thelittlehousecompany.co.uk*) has a basic package for £89. This rate includes a full listing and four photographs. There are no time restrictions, and should you need to change any of the details, you can edit the content of your advert online. For an extra fee (currently £26), this site will place your advert on the 'For sale' pages of some of the largest UK property websites such as Fish4Homes, RightMove and Property Finder, providing a greater chance of attracting a buyer.

If your budget stretches to it you can also include a virtual tour with your advert. There are companies that will film your house for you, or you can do it yourself using a simple webcam. The difference in quality is usually very obvious though, so it may pay to use an expert if you can. E-House (*www.ehouse.co.uk*) and Interactive Tours (*www.interactive-tours.co.uk*) both provide this service throughout the UK. Alternatively, sites such as Houseweb (*www.houseweb.co.uk/vtour*) also provide packages that can include a virtual tour.

Whether you take up a sales package or stick with the free text entries, it pays to market your property with as many sites as possible to increase coverage. To find more private sale sites, take a look at the Move Channel (*www.themovechannel.com*). Access the 'SiteFinder' directory and select the 'Sell/Let – no agent' option.

The legalities

The conveyancing involved when selling a house is less complex than when buying and it is certainly feasible to do it yourself. If this is something that you are considering, take a look at the information provided within the 'How to' section of the Move Channel site (*www.themovechannel.com/howto/sell/diy-conveyancing.asp*).

Renting and letting

You can use the Internet to help you find a property to rent, too. Equally, if you have a property to let you will find opportunities to advertise your property for a small charge or, in some cases, for free.

One helpful site is that of the Association of Residential Lettings Agents (ARLA, *www.arla.co.uk*). Formed in 1981, ARLA is the professional and regulatory body for letting agents in the UK. Members need to demonstrate that they have a thorough knowledge of the profession and are meant to operate within the framework of ethical and professional standards as defined by the association.

The UK Property Shop (*www.ukpropertyshop.co.uk*) is a directory site providing links to letting agents as well as estate agents. The site claims to have details of agents in every town in the UK. You will also find that the majority of sites that sell and purchase property also have sections devoted to rentals. In addition, there are sites dedicated to rentals, such as *www.lettingweb.com*. If you are based in Scotland, try *www.letting-in-scotland.co.uk*, a site claiming over 10,000 visitors each week. In London, *www.net-lettings.co.uk* may provide the answer. Accommodation for Students (*www.accommodationforstudents. com*) is designed specifically for students seeking flats and house-shares. The site allows you to choose a location and searches for all available properties. There is also a chatroom where potential housemates can talk, and a facility to email the landlord.

Moving house

Moving home can be a stressful experience but by organising and planning ahead you can minimise the upheaval. There are Internet sites to help you plan the countdown to the move as well as sites that provide advice and practical help on organising the logistics of the actual move.

Getting ready to move

The I Am Moving (*www.iammoving.com*) website is great for making sure you have remembered to let everyone know about your move. The site provides an electronic form for you to complete and then notifies all the relevant utility companies and businesses, including gas, electricity, telephone and the TV licensing authority, of your move. The Really Moving site (*www.reallymoving.com*) also provides plenty of advice and help with the move. It too allows you to inform businesses and the authorities of your change of address, and has a move planner and reminder feature to help you with the move. Move planners are a godsend if you are likely to forget essentials such as cancelling the milk and the papers, paying the window cleaner and depleting the stocks in the freezer in the run-up to the move.

Moving services

The Really Moving (*www.reallymoving.com*) portal site is excellent for organising the move itself. You can request quotes from removal companies and order packing boxes. Alternatively, look up the web-site of the British Association of Removers (*www.bar.co.uk*) to find a removal company that provides a good level of service. You could also find removal firms in your area by using *www.yell.co.uk*, the online *Yellow Pages*.

Building, converting or renovating a property

Building, conversion or renovation projects require precise planning and management, and the Internet can help with all these areas.

Self-builds

If you cannot find your perfect property you may be tempted to build your own or at least hire an expert to build one for you (see Chapter 11). The first step is to find a suitable plot. Tracking one down can be a difficult as well as time-consuming task, but sites such as *www.buildstore.co.uk/findingland* can help. This site claims to have the UK's largest building-plot database. Described as an essential guide for anyone looking for land, the site is updated daily and all information is verified every five days. There are over 5,000 plots to choose from at any one time. It currently costs £44 for a lifetime membership; for an additional £10 you can register your interest in sharing the purchase of plots with other interested builders.

Alternatively, take a look at one or more of the many self-build *websites* such as *www.selfbuildcentre.com*, *www.selfbuildanddesign.com* or *www.homebuilding.co.uk*. These sites all provide details of plots for sale as well as information and advice for a self-build. In most cases, sites charge for land-search options, although some do provide access to a selection of land and property details free of charge. The ebuild site (*www.ebuild.co.uk*) also includes a handy directory of sites that provide products and services specifically for those building their own property.

Conversions and renovations

The majority of sites providing details of plots for sale also include properties suitable for renovation or conversion. It is certainly worth looking at the sites mentioned in the previous section.

If you are renovating an old property you may want to restore some of the original features. For information on how the Internet can help with restoration projects, see Chapter 11.

Buying property abroad

Buying a house or flat abroad is an attractive prospect whether as a holiday home, a place to retire to or even for investment. Often it is not only the weather that is attractive – prices of property abroad can be quite low too. However, before you jump on the bandwagon it is important to do your research. The laws, taxes and buying procedures can be very different from those of the UK.

Finding an overseas property

Whether buying or selling you may want to ensure that a known and respected body has accredited the company that you are dealing with. The Federation of Overseas Property Developers (*www. fopdac.com*) was founded in 1973 in order to provide a set of standards and ethics. All the members of the federation meet a strict code of practice.

If you have a general interest in foreign property and are looking to compare property prices and availability worldwide, try *www. easier.com* or *www.prestigeproperty.co.uk*. Both sites are easy to navigate and include properties from a range of countries. If your interests lie in a specific country, you will probably find more choice from a specialist site. For example, the World of Florida website (*www. worldofflorida.co.uk*) provides a good starting point for those interested in buying on the Florida coast or inland. Use a search engine to find sites relevant to you by keying in the word 'property' followed by the name of the country you are looking to buy in.

For further advice on international estate agents take a look at the National Association of Estate Agents (*www.naea.co.uk*). The site has a 'Find an agent' option categorised by country.

The buying process

Once you have found your dream property you have the challenge of completing the deal from a distance. If you need to finance your purchase with a mortgage you will need to research the best deals. Whether you are better off with a foreign or a UK mortgage will depend on a number of factors including the interest rates at the time. The Internet can help you track down lenders providing mortgages for overseas properties. Conti Financial (*www.conti-financial.com*) is just one example of a site that provides contacts for overseas mortgages. For more information on mortgages see Chapter 12.

It is certainly recommended that you take expert legal advice when purchasing property abroad. The procedures and legalities can be very different to UK law. Unless you have been personally recommended a foreign solicitor it may be advisable to hire a UK law firm that specialises in overseas purchases. By doing this you overcome the possible problems with language barriers and you have the added advantage of being protected by UK law should you need to claim compensation because of errors on the part of your lawyer. The Internet can help you find a suitable lawyer through sites such as *www.solicitors-online.com*. This Law Society site provides a list of lawyers specialising in foreign law and the legalities of purchasing an overseas property. If you prefer to deal with an expert from the country you are moving to, try Easier2move (*www.easier2move.co.uk*). This site claims to find you a fully qualified, English-speaking lawyer for purchases or sales of overseas properties.

It is not always common practice to carry out a structural survey on an overseas property. However, for your own peace of mind, you may prefer to do so, particularly for older properties. To find a local surveyor you are best to seek personal recommendations or ask the property agent for a list of possible experts.

Chapter 11

Home maintenance

Looking after a home is a full-time job that is all too often squeezed into a few short hours a week. What with keeping it clean, mowing the lawn and making sure that the decorating is up to scratch, finding the time to replace windows or fix the roof can be hard. Unless you are nifty with a toolbox, you will probably need to call on the help of an expert – and the Internet can come to the rescue here. The following sections look at the specific ways in which home-maintenance websites can provide information, advice and services to make life easier for you.

A directory site will point you in the direction of a whole range of related sites, saving you the finger work. A good example of a directory website for home-related needs is the Home and Gardening site (*www.homeandgardening.co.uk*). This provides links to hundreds of quality sites that supply goods and services for the home. Categories include furniture, tools, gardening as well as services such as cleaning. Style Source (*www.stylesource.co.uk*) is a good example of a portal site providing a full range of home and lifestyle information.

Finding tradesmen online

Over the last few years a number of websites have appeared offering lists of tradesmen throughout the UK. In general, these sites provide a free service to you, the customer, and make their revenue through contractor membership fees, commissions and advertising. Some vet their members and others simply provide the details and leave the vetting process to you. The success of these sites ultimately lies with the number of members they have recruited. A website with only a few tradesmen in your area is not going to inspire confidence or provide the necessary choice.

HomePro (*www.homepro.com*) has over 5,000 members. It vets all members for legal and financial problems, insists they offer an insurance-backed guarantee to cover completion of the work should the company cease trading, and requires ten customer references. The members are given a score based on customer feedback that can be viewed on the site.

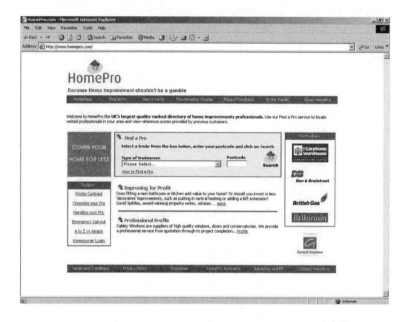

The House website (*www.house.co.uk*) from British Gas offers much more than just information about British Gas services and products. It has a comprehensive service for finding tradespeople that includes a customer rating, credit check and legal check. The site also includes useful DIY advice and solutions.

Accredited tradesmen

There is so much bad press about people being ripped off by cowboy tradesmen that many homeowners are understandably wary of finding 'an expert' by using small ads, *Yellow Pages* or general Internet sites. The industry is keen to improve its reputation and the Internet is paving the way by providing consumers with details of tradesmen who have been vetted and, in many cases, hold industry standard qualifications. The government's Quality Mark Scheme gives you access to independently inspected and approved tradesmen such as builders, roofers, electricians and plumbers. The scheme has been piloted in Birmingham and Somerset and is now being gradually rolled out across the country. Keep an eye on its website, *www.qualitymark.org.uk*, as the database expands.

If the Quality Mark Scheme has not reached your area yet, the best route for tracking down an accredited tradesman is via the websites of the institutes and associations relating to the required trade.

Finding a plumber

The Institute of Plumbing (IoP, *www.plumbers.org.uk*) and the Association of Plumbing and Heating Contractors (APHC, *www.aphc.co.uk*) both have registers of approved members. If you are unhappy with a job carried out by one of their members, both organisations offer a conciliation and arbitration service.

Finding an electrician

Although many homeowners will attempt a whole range of DIY tasks, unless you know what you are doing it is best to leave the electrics to an expert. The National Inspection Council for Electrical Installation Contracting (NICEIC) is the industry's independent body set up to protect consumers against unsound installations. It is definitely worth making sure that any electrician you employ is NICEIC-approved. You can do this by checking on its website (*www.niceic.org.uk*). If you have any concerns about the standard or safety of the work undertaken by one of its members, an inspecting engineer will be sent out to assess the work. If it is found to be unsafe, it will be rectified at no additional cost. The Electrical Contractors' Association (ECA) (*www.eca.co.uk*) also has a stringent assessment in place for members. All members have to pass a technical and commercial inspection and have at least three years of relevant experience within the industry. The members are also bonded, which gives you extra protection if the company you are using goes out of business. Should this happen, another member will complete the work at no extra charge. There is also a warranty in place to cover installation work.

Finding a builder

Building work is customarily accompanied by dust, delays and headaches. A building project without stress is unlikely, but you can improve your chances of getting through the ordeal by using an approved contractor. The Federation of Master Builders (FMB) is the UK's largest trade association, boasting over 14,500 members. Members pay a joining fee and annual subscription and are vetted by existing members from their local branch. Follow-up checks take place only if a complaint is lodged. The FMB also offers a Masterbond guarantee, which costs 1.5 per cent of the contract price. The scheme guarantees the work and materials for ten years and the work will be completed if the contractor becomes bankrupt. For further information and details of members, access *www.fmb. org.uk* and choose the 'Find a builder' section, or alternatively go straight to *www.findabuilder.co.uk*.

The National Federation of Builders (NFB) is another popular trade association for the building industry, with a current membership of around 4,000. Members of the NFB pay an annual subscription and have to provide detailed client, trade and financial references. Members are visited by the NFB and their application is put to a panel of regional member companies for assessment. Once elected as a member the building company will be visited and assessed at least once a year. The NFB offers arbitration and conciliation services and its members can offer customers the Benchmark Plan. This insurance-backed scheme will pay the cost of correcting defects for up to ten years. The NFB website (*www.builders.org.uk*) will provide details of members in your locality.

For specialist tradesmen you may also like to try the Guild of Master Craftsmen (*www.guildmc.com*). This association is not backed by any guarantees, but it does provide a free conciliation service. There are around 15,000 members representing more than 400 trades and crafts. Members pay an annual fee and have to provide five client references.

Finding a roofing contractor
If you are looking for a trade association for roofing contractors try the National Federation of Roofing Contractors (*www.nfrc.co.uk*) or the Confederation of Roofing Contractors (*www.corc.co.uk*). Both associations vet applicants and require evidence that they have the required levels of experience and skill.

Case history

Marie lives in the north of England, a good four-hour drive from her mother, who lives in a village in Norfolk. Since her father died Marie has tried to support her mother from a distance as well as visiting whenever she can. Her mother's property was well maintained while Marie's father was alive but it has since been somewhat neglected, and her mother reported some damp on the chimney-breast in one of the bedrooms. From a similar experience in her own home, Marie assumed that either the chimney needed re-pointing or that the flashings needed replacing. A trip to Norfolk to sort it out was impossible so Marie decided to try to organise a builder from a distance.

'My biggest concern was landing Mum with a cowboy. You hear of so many cases where a builder goes up on the roof and comes back down with horror stories and estimates for thousands of pounds. I decided to try and find a reputable builder; even if they proved more expensive I would be assured that their estimate was for legitimate work.

'I went on the Find a Builder site (*www.findabuilder.co.uk*) and typed in Mum's postcode. It came up with a choice of only two but that gave me a good starting point. I phoned them both and explained the situation. I arranged for them to visit the house at a time when I knew Mum would be out and then email the quote directly to me. Both builders came up with the same diagnosis, which was reassuring and the quotes where similar. With little to choose between the two I plumped for the cheaper one, and organised for the work to take place while Mum was staying with me.

'I would certainly use the Internet again to find tradesmen but I would use only sites on which the members had been vetted and hold industry standard accreditations.'

Finding a gas installer

Faulty gas appliances, servicing and installation result in deaths every year. It is dangerous (and illegal) to tackle problems with gas appliances yourself, so if you have any concerns it is vital to call in an expert. Anyone carrying out work on gas installations or appliances must be registered with the Council for Registered Gas Installers (CORGI). To find a registered CORGI engineer in your area, access *www.corgi-gas.co.uk*.

Gardening and landscaping

Whether you garden as a profession, maintain your own garden or simply enjoy pottering around, the Internet will have a site to suit you. Even if you are an armchair (or deckchair) gardener the Internet can help you find someone to keep your weeds and lawn in check while inspiring you with images of beautifully landscaped gardens and exotic plants.

Advice and information

If you are a subscriber to Which? Online (*www.which.net*) you need look no further. *Gardening Which?* is packed full of ideas, expert advice as well as solutions to gardening problems. The Crocus website (*www.crocus.co.uk*) is attractive and informative with a comprehensive range of services including a plant search, up-to-date gardening news and design advice. This award-winning site by Alan Titchmarsh is both professional and slick and is well worth a look. Another site that is definitely worth spending time exploring is the BBC's site (*www.bbc.co.uk/gardening*). As with all the offerings from the BBC, its gardening section is hard to beat. The virtual garden planner is a fun addition to the site enabling you to create your own virtual garden. Gardening UK (*www.gardening-uk.co.uk*) is another useful site.

If you find pleasure in nurturing your garden you may enjoy the Real Gardeners website (*www.realgardeners.co.uk*). This is a community site set up by UK gardeners to exchange tips, ideas and even seeds. The All 4 Gardens (*www.all4gardens.com*) website has a resident expert to answer all your gardening queries. The 'Ask Ned' section aims to provide an answer to your question within 48 hours. Ned also has a colleague, Sue, who will help with any landscaping challenges. Carry on Gardening (*www. carryongardening.org.uk*) is another great site, packed full of hints, tips and good ideas.

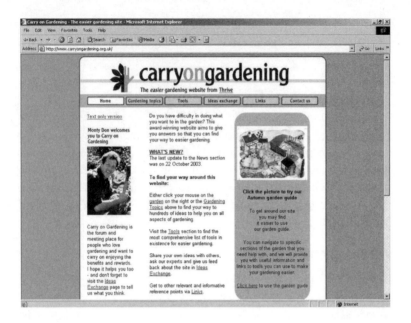

Buying online

There are plenty of shopping sites dedicated to the needs of the gardener. For a full range of sites try *www.gardenmagazine.com*. Part of Shopping.Net, this site provides a directory of websites catering for the gardener. The site also links to eBay (*www.ebay. co.uk*), the auction site for those who want to pick up a second-hand lawnmower or two, as well as a host of sites providing gardening services, advice and products. This is a good place to start if you are browsing. If you are specifically looking to buy plants or seeds, Gardening UK (*www.gardening-uk.com*, not to be confused with *www.gardening-uk.co.uk* mentioned above) provides a directory of catalogues from bulbs and seeds through to exotic plants for conservatories. The site also provides information on garden-related services and products including landscaping, garden furniture and books. If it is tools you are after, try Tooled Up (*www.tooled-up.com*). This is a shopping site specialising in providing a full range of gardening implements. For furniture, try *www.garden-furniture-uk.com*.

Bringing in the experts

If gardening is not your cup of tea and you would rather pay someone to do it for you try the British Association of Landscape Industries (BALI, *www.bali.co.uk*). This site will help you find a residential gardener based in your area. Alternatively, use a search engine to look for sites with the word 'gardener' followed by your town or region. You should be able to find some local expertise as well as further national sites that provide this service.

Restoration, DIY and interior design

Whether it is putting up shelves, stencilling the hallway or making curtains, most of us have had a go at doing it ourselves. Some take to it like a duck to water while others seem to court disaster. Our fascination with home improvement is clearly evident from the number of TV programmes dedicated to the subject.

If you are one of the millions of people who turn to television property programmes for advice and inspiration you will enjoy the property pages of the Channel 4 website (*www.channel4.com/4homes*) and the BBC website (*www.bbc.co.uk/homes/property*). Both sites provide topical and up-to-date information on trends and new developments in the property world as well as tips on how to make the most of your property. They also keep you informed of the full range of current and forthcoming property programmes.

With the wealth of information and advice available, the Internet is sure to provide inspiration regardless of whether you are a DIY expert or an armchair enthusiast.

Restoration

Restoring a home to its former glory can be a time-consuming and expensive business. Unless you are an expert, the first step will undoubtedly involve research. This is where the Internet can prove invaluable. Instead of spending hours at the local library poring over history books, you can research the original period features, the materials, fabrics and colours without moving from your own home.

For specific research use an Internet search engine and search on the relevant terms, for example 'Victorian fireplaces'. For general information on period decoration try the British Interior Design Association (BIDA, *www.bida.org*) or *www.buildingconservation.com*, the online version of the Building Conservation Directory. Sites such as *www.heritage.co.uk* and *www.english-heritage.org.uk* may also provide inspiration. If you are a private owner of a heritage house, the Historic Houses Association (*www.hha.org.uk*) can prove a useful source of information.

If the original features have been stripped you will need to source replacements. Rather than traipsing around the country in search of that elusive Victorian toilet cistern, try *www.salvo.co.uk*. This site provides a search facility to find salvage yards, antique outlets and specialist retailers in your area.

If your project requires the expertise of an architect, you may find a local specialist through searching the Register of Architects Accredited in Building Conservation (*www.aabc-register.co.uk*). If you need practical help with the restoration work, contact the Federation of Master Builders (*www.fmb.org.uk*) and search for a builder with experience in restoring properties from the same period as yours.

DIY stores and retail sites

Most of the larger DIY stores have their own sites providing shopping online as well as advice and tips. Three of the most well known are Homebase (*www.homebase.co.uk*), B&Q (*www.diy.com*) and Focus (*www.focusdoitall.co.uk*). Before you buy, remember to stick to the guidelines recommended in Chapter 7.

It is worth comparing prices with sites that do not have high street outlets. Decorating Direct (*www.decoratingdirect.co.uk*) is a virtual hardware shop that claims to sell direct to the public at trade prices. The site lacks the levels of advice and hand-holding that can be found on other sites but it makes up for this by being easy and quick to navigate. Delivery is free if you spend more than £50.

The DIY Fix It site (*www.diyfixit.co.uk*) is brilliant for DIY tips. The advice is straightforward and easy to follow. The BBC website also has a useful DIY section (*www.bbc.co.uk/homes/diy/diy_guide*) where you can ask the experts for help.

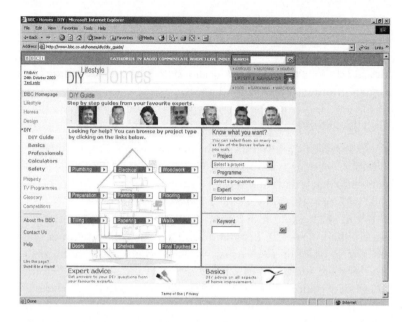

Decorating

Decorating a room can often involve weeks of deliberation and research before the paint even touches the brush. It is often difficult to imagine the finished room and even with the aid of numerous tester pots it is hard to decide on the best colours. There are websites that can help. The Dulux site (*www.dulux.com*) is full of practical decorating advice and colour inspiration. Select the 'UK DIY' option to try out the Mouse Painter. This innovative tool allows you to paint rooms online to see whether your colour choices for walls, floors and furniture will look great or grim. Once you have found your perfect combination you can print out the end result along with paint references. If you select the 'UK Dulux decorator centre' from the home page you will find advice on paints, wall coverings and accessories. And if decorating isn't really your thing, select 'Dulux trade' from the home page and then choose the 'Homeowners' option. You will be presented with an option to find a local decorator to do it all for you.

Paint Quality (*www.paintquality.co.uk*) is an excellent site for finding out everything that you need to know about painting. There are step-by-step instructions from preparation through to the finishing coat. There is also a problem-solver and a calculator that helps you work out exactly how much paint you will need for the job. If you enjoy stencilling, try Stencil Planet *www.stencilplanet.com* or the Stencil Library *www.stencil-library.com*. Both sites include online catalogues offering thousands of designs.

Interior design

If you are short on inspiration for interior design, Home Interiors (*www.homeinteriors.co.uk*) may provide a few ideas. This site's mission states that it will supply all its customers with top-quality products, with next-day delivery at up to half the retail price.

If you are looking to fill your home with stylish furniture you can use the Internet for inspiration and, if your budget permits, you can always order an item or two online. As a starting point, try a directory site such as *www.somucheasier.co.uk* and select the 'Home and garden' option. This site provides direct links to the websites of many of the high street furniture retailers, department stores as well as home-furnishing outlets. For individual design, take a look at the Interior Internet site (*www.interiorinternet.com*) or use a search engine and search on the words 'designer furniture'.

Home management

Day-to-day home management can be an exhausting and often thankless task. So can the Internet take the pain out of shopping, gardening, cleaning and paying the bills? It can help save you time and remove some of the tedium.

Supermarket shopping

Unless you enjoy your weekly supermarket shop think seriously about shopping online. For a fee of around £5 (or in some cases free) you can get all your groceries from an online supermarket delivered straight to your door. By shopping online you will probably save more than the delivery fee on impulse buys, as well as saving on parking fees and petrol. For more information and a case study describing an online supermarket shopping experience, see Chapter 7.

Paying for utilities

The costs for utilities such as gas, electricity and telephone can be high. With deregulation, these areas have been opened up to competition and you have probably been bombarded with offers for reducing your bills. 'Switch with Which?', a campaign by *Which?*, has a website (*www.switchwithwhich.co.uk*) that provides you with calculators to help you work out the best deal based on your usage. For further details, see Chapter 12.

Cleaning and housework

For many, housework is a chore. The Internet can provide help in finding practical assistance but if your budget will not stretch to paying for a cleaner you will still find tips to make the job easier and save you time. For a site that will make you smile, try *www.flylady.net*. Designed not to be taken too seriously, this American site has some very good tips.

Employing a cleaner can be stressful. Many people are uncomfortable with the idea of a stranger being in their home and are concerned about security issues as well as coping with a service that does not meet expectations. As with all services, recommendation is the best way of choosing a cleaner, but if you cannot find someone this way you might like to try one of the Internet sites dedicated to providing home helps.

To find a local, independent cleaner, try the Find a Cleaner website (*www.findacleaner.org*). This site provides a national register of domestic cleaners. The companies and individuals registered are not vetted by the website so you will need to check references. If you still have no joy, use a search engine and search on the words 'domestic cleaner' followed by your town or area. This should find local cleaning companies as well as further national registers.

If you are looking for an expert to clean carpets or soft furnishings, try the National Carpet Cleaners' Association (*www.ncca.co.uk*). Alternatively, Clean Care GB Ltd (*www.cleancare.co.uk*) provides national operators to clean floors, floor coverings, upholstery, curtains and windows. To help with kitchen grime, *www.ovenclean.com* will clean your cooker without fuss or mess.

If you have de-cluttered your home only to find you have a pile of items to get rid of, try *www.wastepoint.co.uk*. Part of Waste

Connect, this site provides a database for every recycling facility in the country from paper, tins and glass to toys and furniture. Take a look at the site to find your nearest recycling point.

Chapter 12

Personal finance

The marketplace is overflowing with financial offerings, and finding a suitable product is a daunting task. Traditionally it is a case of ringing around or visiting financial institutions and gathering together all the product brochures. Then comes the difficult job of comparing products, not an easy task when they all have slightly different features. Help is always at hand from independent financial advisors (IFAs), who will track down the best product based on your requirements. Alternatively, you can always carry out your own research either by using the comparative tables and money facts available from publications such as *Which?* or you can harness the wealth of information available on the Internet. With the growing trend for financial institutions to offer their products over the Net, there is now so much information available for purchasers of financial products. E-finance has well and truly arrived.

What is e-finance?

E-finance is the ability to research and purchase financial services electronically, via the Internet. It is true to say that the uptake of e-finance has been slower than that of some other services on the Net. This is partly because of concerns about security but it has also been held back for legal considerations. Many of these concerns and legal issues have now been addressed by the industry, but e-finance cannot be considered to be 'truly electronic' until there is a process for signing online on the dotted line. Although the legal structure and the technicalities for this are in place and doubtless it will happen, the issue of money-laundering regulations needs to be considered. These regulations make it necessary for documents to be delivered by post or in person in order to confirm identity when you first take up most financial products.

Legalities apart, the Internet undoubtedly brings power to the consumer. Not only does it give you financial control, it also provides a constant supply of updated information, news and statistics. So, even if you are not confident about buying a financial product online you can still research the products before seeking professional advice. If you do decide to take the plunge and buy a product online you will find that the process is greatly simplified by the services of financial comparison websites. These sites typically provide a comparison of providers and their products. This means that you can start your research by searching a database of providers to find the best deals based on your personal requirements. This narrows down the field and you can then visit only the sites of the companies providing the best deals.

By buying a financial product online you can often save yourself some money. By selling online, direct to the customer, financial product providers do not have to pay sales staff or pay commission to a middleman. Some organisations pass on savings to the customer by offering more competitively priced products but, as with offline deals, not all online offers are competitive, so it pays to shop around first.

Tip

It is always worth trying several financial comparison sites as some are far from comprehensive. Compare the results you get from one of them with those produced by the Financial Services Authority (FSA, *www.fsa.gov.uk*). The FSA regulates financial firms in the UK, and its site provides a useful and impartial source of information. For some products the site also provides similar services to the commercial sites through its own comparative tables.

Safety and security

A number of surveys have shown that consumers are wary when it comes to purchasing financial services over the Internet. These concerns have been fuelled by high-profile news stories of things

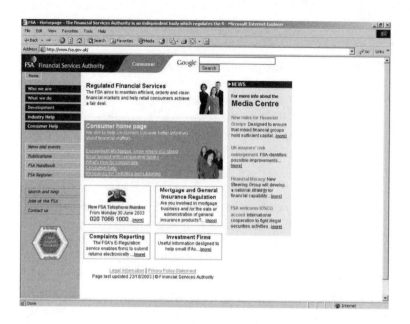

going wrong, but it is important to put these incidents into perspective and consider the wider picture.

Protection

The laws that protect you when you purchase financial products from the high street or by telephone equally apply when you buy online. There is also additional reassurance from the Distance Marketing of Consumer Financial Services Directive that came into force in October 2002 and is to be implemented by September 2004. The directive applies to any 'distance contract' involving financial services and includes a clause allowing the consumer to withdraw from a contract without penalty and without giving any reason for a period of 14 calendar days after buying the product. This period is extended to 30 calendar days in distance contracts relating to life insurance and personal pensions. There are some exclusions to this clause (relating to areas such as foreign exchange) and it is worth checking the full details of the directive if you have concerns. You can print a copy from the HM Treasury site (*www.hm-treasury. gov.uk/consultations_and_legislation/dmd/consult_dmd_index.cfm*).

Further protection is afforded by the Financial Services and Markets Act 2000, which came into force at the end of 2001. It made

> **Buy wisely**
>
> If you seek professional advice and that advice is subsequently found to be inappropriate, the law affords you some comeback. However, the law will not provide any protection if you do not take advice and buy a product that proves to be unsuitable. This is certainly more likely to happen if you buy online, so think carefully before you commit yourself.

the Financial Services Authority (FSA, *www.fsa.gov.uk*) the regulator for much of the financial services industry, with a remit to maintain market confidence in the UK financial system. The FSA is charged with promoting public awareness as well as protecting consumers and reducing financial crime.

The Banking Code is also designed to protect consumers whether they bank at the high street or online. Most recently updated in March 2003, the code now contains standards that cover how banks should deal with requests from current-account customers who want to switch banks. It also provides standards covering areas such as how to run your account, interest rates, charges and terms and conditions, and dealing with financial difficulties.

For further information on the code, take a look at the Banking Code Standards Board's website (*www.bankingcode.org.uk*) or you can view or download a copy from the British Banker's Association site (*www.bba.org.uk*). It is important to note that not all financial institutions subscribe to this code.

Complaints about financial services

If you have a complaint concerning a financial organisation or an individual broker the first step should always be to complain to the firm. If this does not work you can contact the Financial Ombudsman Scheme (*www.financial-ombudsman.org.uk*) or other relevant complaints bodies such as the General Insurance Standards Council (*www.gisc.co.uk*) to help resolve the issue.

The Financial Services and Markets Act established the Financial Services Compensation Scheme (FSCS, *www.fscs.org.uk*). The scheme operates by charging participating firms fees; this money is then used to pay compensation. The FSCS is authorised to pay compensation to consumers if they have lost out financially because of a firm's negligence or fraud and the firm has become insolvent. Claiming compensation does not require any form of professional representation.

Helping yourself

The majority of financial firms must be authorised by the FSA or specifically exempt from authorisation before they can do business in the UK. Before you deal with any financial firm it is advisable to ensure that it is authorised by the FSA and that it subscribes to the Banking Code. You can check FSA membership by using the FSA's Firm Check service (*www.fsa.gov.uk/consumer*). If a company is listed you can be confident that:

- the organisation has been vetted and is competent, honest and solvent
- the organisation conducts its business in accordance with the rules set out by the FSA
- you have access to a complaints procedure run by the firm and by way of the Financial Ombudsman Scheme
- you may be able to claim compensation from the Financial Services Compensation Scheme.

It is also worth checking that the company provides a UK address or a telephone number should you need to contact it. Be wary of firms that provide phone numbers that start with the digits 09 because these calls will be charged at a premium rate.

You may find that some firms are classified as an 'appointed representative' of another firm. Provided that the firm it represents is authorised you are still fully protected.

Buying financial services from abroad

The Internet opens up a whole world of opportunities and you may be tempted to consider financial offerings from foreign sources. Non-UK organisations are not allowed to tout for your business unless they are from a country in the European Economic Area (EEA) or have been given special permission by the FSA. If you do track down a product from the website of a foreign provider there is nothing to stop you buying but it is important to remember that you will not be protected by the FSA should something go wrong. Before you buy, it is worth finding out what level of protection you will get from the country of origin.

If you buy from a European Union country that is selling services to UK customers you should be able to pursue any legal action though the UK court system if you find yourself in dispute. Firms from the EEA are, as mentioned above, allowed to operate in the UK without being authorised by the FSA, but they are still regulated by their home country or country of origin.

Which? advises consumers not to buy from organisations that do not have FSA authorisation. This is sound advice as it is often difficult to determine whether the firm is operating under regulations that you consider acceptable.

Security

Whether you are buying financial services or any other goods over the Internet the same security issues apply. It is important to make sure that the site has a security policy and is secure whenever you are sending personal information or credit-card details. A secure site can be identified by an address that begins 'https://' and a secure page should be identified by a closed padlock or key usually displayed at the bottom of the screen. You also need to be sure that the information you provide is stored securely. Companies storing confidential data are required, by law, to hold the information behind a firewall or on a computer that is not linked to the Internet. A firewall is a security measure that protects sensitive information that is held on a computer linked to the Internet. For more information on site security, see Chapter 7.

Privacy

Financial agreements often involve the divulgence of sensitive and personal information. Before you enter this information you should be assured that the information will not be used for any purpose other than that stated. The Data Protection Act 1998 gives you certain rights, and if organisations breach those rights they are breaking the law and can be fined.

Reputable organisations will include a privacy policy on their site. It is advisable to read it carefully and print a copy before you provide any confidential information.

Terms and conditions

Before you sign up for any financial service it is always important to scrutinise the terms and conditions. When you are buying from a salesperson, broker or financial advisor he or she is obliged to point out the terms and conditions and you can discuss any points that are not clear. If you are buying over the Internet the onus is on you to make sure you have read and understood the small print.

Tip

It is easy for organisations to change their terms and conditions on the Internet so make sure you print out a copy of the version that you have committed to.

Online banking

The nature of banking has changed tremendously over the last decade or so. Banking has become depersonalised and some customers have become disillusioned with the new range of services on offer, demanding that traditional branch banking be maintained. However, although this resistance is in evidence, the telephone and Internet are gradually becoming the accepted mode for twenty-first century banking, particularly by younger customers. It is estimated that 10.4 million people in the UK have registered for an online banking service, although surveys suggest that around 50 per cent of those who have registered to bank online have never actually used the service.

How to choose an online bank

Almost all banks and building societies now offer some form of online banking service. There is also a range of Internet-only banks to choose from, enticing you with offers of higher interest rates for current and savings accounts. It is very much a case of shopping around and finding a bank that suits you. Switching banks has become easier so it is worth considering all the options. If you haven't decided whether to stick with your current bank or to sign up for one of the new online-only banks, try out the demonstrations on some of the banking services on the Net to see what is most convenient for you.

To find out the web address of your bank, use a search engine and search on the bank's name. If you are interested in looking at some of the Internet-only banks, type the keywords 'Internet bank' into the search box and put a tick in the UK-only box to limit the search. You should find a full range, including the following Internet-only banks: Cahoot (*www.cahoot.com*), Egg (*www.egg.com*), Smile (*www.smile.co.uk*), Intelligent Finance (*www.if.com*) and ING Direct (*www.ingdirect.co.uk*).

Tip

Whether you choose to bank online or use an alternative method, the Internet can still help you get the best deal. Research shows that the majority of customers stick with the same bank for years without really considering whether they are happy with the service that they are receiving. With this in mind, *Which?* has launched the 'Switch with Which' campaign (*www.switchwithwhich.co.uk*) to help consumers find out whether they could get a better deal and better service elsewhere, be it with an online or a high street bank.

If you do decide to change banks, the new version of the Banking Code states that your current bank must provide your new bank with information about your standing orders and direct debits within three days of your request. This can take some of the legwork out of making the change. Further details can be found at *www.bankingcode.org.uk*.

How does online banking work?

With Internet banking you access your account through your bank's website. You will need a computer, modem and an Internet Service Provider (ISP). You may also find that you need to have up-to-date anti-virus software installed on your PC. You can always check with your bank to make sure that the specification of your equipment is adequate.

When you register with a bank you will be given a login code and a password. It is important that you keep this information to yourself and do not write it down anywhere obvious. You will also probably be advised to change this information on a regular basis.

Passwords

Never divulge your login code or password to anyone over the phone. There have been occasions when someone has phoned a customer pretending to be an official from the bank and has asked the customer for his or her login code and password for identification purposes. A valid caller from a bank will never ask for this information, so on no account divulge it. If you have any concerns at all regarding the authenticity of a caller, ask for his or her name and call back using a phone number that you are sure is valid.

Egg has developed a Money Manager Service in an attempt to make banking online easier. Many of those who bank online have accounts with several different banks. This results in several sets of passwords to access their accounts. The idea behind Egg's Money Manager Service is to allow the user to access all their accounts in the one place using the same password. However, you should check with your financial provider that by using this service you are not breaking the conditions of your account, because if money is taken from your account you could be liable for the losses.

One of the major advantages of online banking has to be the flexibility. You can bank 24 hours a day, seven days a week, although if you bank in the middle of the night, the bank is unlikely to deal with your request until the next day. You can also look at the status of your finances at any time, calling up online statements and account balances. Most banks also allow you to transfer money between your accounts, set up direct debits and transfer money to other UK accounts. The facilities available do differ from bank to bank and it is a good idea to make a list of all the things that you usually do at your branch and make sure that the majority of these facilities are available from the online bank that you choose.

The way in which you pay money in and take money out of your account will differ depending on the online bank you choose. If you use an online bank or building society with a high street presence the process is just the same as for non-online banking. You will be able to pay money in at a branch, either in person or by using a credit-posting box outside the bank, and you can get money out from the branch or by using a cash machine.

If you plump for an Internet-only bank, paying in arrangements vary. Smile, for instance, has arranged for post offices to accept cash or cheque payments, whereas some other banks will accept cheques only if they are sent by post. To withdraw cash from an Internet-only bank you can use cash machines, and many also provide cheque book facilities.

The cashless society

The development of online banking is moving us further towards the cashless society. With this aim in mind, Cahoot has recently launched a virtual credit card for use on the Internet. The webcard is available to all current account or credit-card holders and can be downloaded in just a few minutes. Security is obviously a major issue but to overcome this the webcard generates a unique 16-digit number every time a transaction takes place. This prevents someone obtaining the card number and using it fraudulently.

The webcard can be activated by entering the usual security details on the bank's website. An icon is then set up on the PC and when you want to spend you simply click on the icon to bring up the webcard. The webcard details can be dragged and dropped into the checkout section of any e-commerce site, and each time the number will be altered. If you are interested in finding out more about this new technology take a look at the Cahoot website (*www.cahoot.com*). As well as finding more information you can also view an online demonstration. To keep abreast of other banks offering this or similar services, search on the keyword 'webcard'.

Another major development in the pipeline is the use of smartcards. These are plastic cards that contain a computer chip. The idea is that you will be able to slot your smartcard into your PC and download electronic cash from your bank account on to the card.

The card can then be used for small purchases from shops or other establishments that have a smartcard reader. When the card is running low, you simply top it up.

Borrowing online

There are so many financial institutions eager to lend you money it is difficult to determine what is the best deal. Instead of traipsing around from bank to building society it is often more convenient to do the groundwork by reading the personal finance sections of newspapers or reviewing financial surveys such as those provided by *Which?*. Alternatively, you can use the Internet to make comparisons easily. Online surveys and comparison tables can often prove superior to more traditional research routes – they are convenient to access and up to date, and often allow you to base your research on specific factors. By using the Internet you can at least narrow down the choice even if you do not end up buying online.

Mortgages

The first step is to do your research. If you know the facts you are less likely to be sold something unsuitable. Most mortgage websites have information pages that include a guide to home-buying or remortgaging as well as a jargon-busting glossary. You are likely to find useful guidance from sites that provide product comparisons, such as Interactive Investor/Ample (*www.iii.co.uk*), FT Your Money (*www.ftyourmoney.com*), Moneyfacts (*www.moneyfacts.co.uk*) and Charcol Online (*www.charcolonline.co.uk*). For impartial information, try the Which? Mortgage Search (*www.switchwithwhich.co.uk*). It's an interactive mortgage search which gives you access to a constantly updated database of over 8,000 mortgage products, and finds the best deals for you based on the criteria you enter, whether you're a first-time buyer or are looking to switch lenders. It offers a unique combination of comprehensive market coverage, comparison of mortgages on total costs and a switching facility which shows you whether you could save any money by moving to a different deal. Alongside the search there's lots of Which? information about mortgages and what to look out for when you're getting one.

Another impartial site to try is the FSA's (*www.fsa.gov.uk/tables*). This site is not as user friendly as some of the others but it is worth taking a look and comparing products before purchasing from another site. For further sites, use a search engine and search on the keywords 'mortgage information'.

Once you have completed your research and you know what you are looking for, the next step is to take a look at a few mortgage-comparison sites. These sites provide a good starting point if you are shopping around for a mortgage, with the majority providing a database of products that you can search based on your own requirements. For example, you may want a flexible mortgage that enables you to pay off lump sums with no penalty, or you may want to be able to rent your property, or you may be purchasing abroad. By stating your requirements you can narrow down the field considerably.

Once you have found a product that fits your requirements take some time to read the small print. It is also worth making sure that you are buying from a reputable organisation. The majority of mortgage lenders and many advisors subscribe to the Mortgage Code, a set of standards for good practice. For further information visit *www.mortgagecode.co.uk*.

Case history

Ali and Nina have recently married and are looking to take out their first mortgage. They both bank online and have also taken out car insurance online so searching for a mortgage using the Internet does not faze them at all.

Ali says, 'We decided to try a site recommended to us by a friend. The site gives you the option to choose and buy your mortgage online, over the phone or face to face. If you decide to use the online option there is an online wizard that you can work through to help you find the mortgage that best suits your circumstances. The good thing is that if you sort it out yourself you don't pay any broker fees. But, if you do get stuck, you can always give them a call and they'll put you in touch with one of their independent financial advisers.

'We clicked on the 'Online wizard' option and then selected 'First time buyer'. It was then just a case of working through the questions. We wanted to borrow £95,000 over 25 years and we had decided to plump for a repayment mortgage. As we were looking for a joint mortgage we had to both enter details of our age, salary and any debts we have. Once we had worked through the questions, which took only a few minutes, the site came up with 307 suitable mortgages!

'To cut down the options we selected to answer some advanced questions. We were not worried about the type of mortgage but we were keen to be able to pay off lump sums, without penalty, if and when we have spare cash. We also did not want to have to buy the insurance products from the mortgage provider as Nina works for an insurance company and can get discounted products.

'Once we had worked through this next set of questions, which again took only a couple of minutes, the site provided a more manageable list of suitable mortgages. The first two on the list were flagged as best buys, one from Intelligent Finance and the other from Scottish Widows. We have set aside next weekend to do some more research on some of the mortgages that have been recommended. At first glance the terms look really good.'

Tip

For sensible advice on using credit, try the Office of Fair Trading (*www.oft.gov.uk*) website. If you do get into unmanageable debt, it is advisable not to bury your head. You can find advice and help at the National Debtline (*www.nationaldebtline.co.uk*), the Consumer Credit Counselling Service (*www.cccs.co.uk*),or your local Citizens Advice Bureau (*www.nacab.org.uk*). You can also find a money advisor or lawyer who can help with debt problems through the Community Legal Service (*www.justask.org.uk*). *Life After Debt*, published by Which? Books, offers practical guidance on this subject.

Loans

For general guidance on borrowing take a look at some of the product-comparison sites (such as *www.moneyfacts.co.uk*) mentioned in the section on mortgages.

The majority of lenders offer their services through a branch or by phone, post or the Internet. There are also some lenders who are purely Internet-based. If you are shopping around, start your search by using a product-comparison site (see *Mortgages*). You will usually be required to complete a questionnaire that will be analysed online. You will then be presented with a list of financial institutions that would be prepared to grant you a loan along with the rates they are offering. You will usually find that the cheapest option is listed first.

Investing online

Investors can now manage their own financial portfolio of investments online. You can buy and sell stocks and shares, sort out your own Individual Savings Accounts (ISAs) and research the best deals in pensions. Although you have all this power at your fingertips you must be aware that there is no legal comeback if you buy an unsuitable product without having taken professional advice.

Stocks and shares

Most online brokers are execution-only: they will buy and sell on your behalf but they will not offer advice based on your specific circumstances. The majority of sites provide some information on the market as a whole and can even offer some share tips but, basically, if you are going to dabble on the stock exchange, online, you need to know what you are doing. You will also find that many of the broker sites provide basic information free of charge to attract you to the site but also provide additional services, at a price. For instance, if you are a subscriber to a site you can often view real-time share price changes, whereas non-subscribers are likely to see prices that are 15 minutes or so out of date.

For a list of online brokers try the London Stock Exchange site (*www.londonstockexchange.com*). Ask friends if they can recommend a broker, but if you need to shop around for an Internet stock-broker try FT Your Money (*www.ftyourmoney.com*). Both have options for comparing the services provided by online brokers. For a full range of sites, search on the keywords 'Internet stockbroker'.

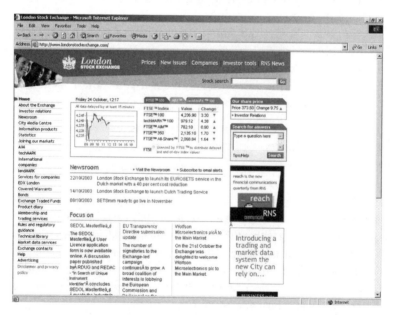

Investments

Although buying and selling shares is the most popular online investment activity, you can also purchase investment funds (either within or outside of an ISA wrapper).

217

The cheapest and most convenient way to track down an investment fund is through a fund supermarket – a single website where you can browse the funds offered by a range of different providers and, importantly, invest in funds from several providers within a single ISA.

Before selecting a fund supermarket, consider the following:

- decide which particular funds you want to buy, and from which fund managers
- find the supermarkets offering the best prices on those funds
- consider a wider choice of funds and fund managers, in case you want to switch later
- if there are several supermarkets that look good, consider other services. For example, do they provide background information on funds and fund managers?
- check that you can look at your investments and manage your account online
- find out whether the supermarket will accept your old PEPs and ISAs
- check that it will let you switch to another supermarket. If it will, find out the costs you will incur if you want to switch or close your account.

To find a range of online fund supermarkets, use a search engine and search on the keywords 'fund supermarket'.

Tip

Supermarkets sell funds on an execution-only basis, which means you are investing without the help of a financial adviser. Basically, if you buy the wrong thing, there is no one to blame but yourself. However, if you choose the fund supermarket wisely and make sure that it is registered with the FSA, you still have rights to protection if it goes bust or gives you bad service.

Pensions

Pensions can be complicated and traditionally have been sold by salespeople and agents tied to product providers or by independent financial advisors. With the introduction of the stakeholder pension, finding a pension to suit your circumstances is a less complex task. With no hidden costs and an annual management fee limited to 1 per cent, the stakeholder pension is a relatively simple product to sell directly to the consumer online. But however simple the purchase may be, individual circumstances need to be addressed, and the majority of consumers are best advised to use the Internet as a source of information, seeking professional advice before parting with their money.

If you want to find out more about stakeholder pensions, visit the OPAS stakeholder helpline (*www.stakeholderhelpline.org.uk*). For general, impartial information on pensions, try the government's website (*www.pensionguide.gov.uk*).

There are many commercial sites queuing up to sell you a pension. Comparison sites will display tables of information allowing you to compare rival products. The majority also provide a useful feature to enable you to work out exactly how much you need to contribute to reach your required level of income in retirement. To find a range of sites use a search engine to search on keywords such as 'personal pensions'. You could try *www.moneyfacts.co.uk* or *www.moneyextra.com* as a starting point; both sites access a wide range of financial products including pensions. Compare the information with a few other sites before selecting a product, and remember, unless you really know what you are doing, take advice before signing up for anything.

Tip

Before you sign up for a pension it is worth finding out exactly how much your state pension might be worth at retirement age. You can do this by accessing the Department for Work and Pensions website (*www.dwp.gov.uk*) and completing form BR19.

Insurance online

Before you start your online search for an insurance provider, look for some background information on the types of policies available and the cover they provide. Try the website of the

Association of British Insurers (ABI, *www.insurance.org.uk*) and select the 'Consumer' option. Alternatively, visit the General Insurance Standards Council's site (*www.gisc.gov.uk*) for a guide to the service you should expect from insurance advisors.

Armed with the relevant information the next step is to see what is on offer. If you have a provider in mind, you can go directly to its site, fill in an online form and receive an instant quote. It may pay to do some shopping around and visit a number of product-comparison sites. There are a number of comparison sites specific to insurance, many of which are run by brokers, so you can also buy online. Use a search engine and search for keywords such as 'insurance online' for a selection of sites, or try *www.insurancewide.com* or *www.screentrade.co.uk* as a starting point. Both sites allow you to compare the results from a range of different insurers and also see details of the policies. Alternatively, the FIND website (*www.find.co.uk*) provides a directory that caters for a wide range of insurance needs.

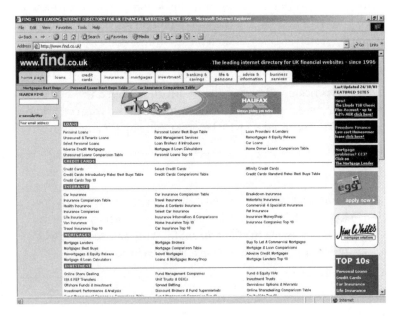

> **Tip**
>
> Product-comparison sites do not always include a full range of products for every type of insurance. So, even if you have found a favourite site that has provided a good deal for one type of insurance do not assume that it will also come up with the best offering for a different kind of insurance product. It is always worth visiting a number of comparison sites and comparing results.

Financial information and advice online

Researching financial information has never been so easy. The majority of financial sites provide some background information and up-to-date market news, but when it comes to seeking financial advice, the Internet is not so forthcoming.

Financial news and trends

A number of sites provide financial news coverage, trends and statistics. For example, Blays (*www.blays.co.uk*) has provided financial information for national newspapers, banks, building societies and financial institutions for 20 years, and it has now made the data available over the Internet.

The Financial Times has a range of websites that can be accessed directly or through *www.ft.com*. Ftyourmoney (*www.ftyourmoney. co.uk*) is the comprehensive personal finance site, providing useful information on topics such as tax and benefits, pensions, ISAs and mortgages. FT Market Watch (*www.ftmarketwatch.com*) provides the lowdown on the financial markets and City news. *The Guardian*'s offering can be found at *www.guardian.co.uk/money*. It is a useful source of news-based financial information. As an alternative, try *www.money. telegraph.co.uk*, part of *The Daily Telegraph*'s website, or *www.economist. com*, *The Economist*'s website. If you are keeping up with the stock exchange, visit the Reuters site (*www.reuters.com*) for all the latest news.

Financial advice online

In the main, e-finance sites are geared for those who know what they want. But if you are in need of advice, you could try the services of the independent financial advisors (IFAs) who operate online. If you decide to do so, you will usually be asked to complete a detailed online questionnaire, which will then be analysed. The response you receive will be based on the information you have provided and it will be forwarded to you by email. At the time of writing there appears to be no central directory of IFAs that provide an online service, but this is likely to change. In the meantime, if you search on the keywords 'financial advisor online', you will find some matches. The one that crops up with most search engines is AdviceOnline (*www.adviceonline.co.uk*). Launched in 1997, this was one of the first independent money websites to offer regulated independent financial advice online. Advice is given by telephone, email and written report, with face-to-face meetings only when requested. Regulated by the FSA, this site offers advice via its parent company, Park Row Group plc, which employs over 300 IFAs.

If you find other online IFAs, make sure that they are registered with the FSA before you consider using them. Alternatively, until there is more choice, it may be advisable to stick with face-to-face advice. Try the Society of Financial Advisors' site (*www.sofa.org*) for a list of IFAs qualified to at least Advanced Financial Planning Certificate level, which is a higher qualification than the minimum standard required for all IFAs. The site allows you to search by location, area of business and the type of charge levied by the IFA. Alternatively, for a directory of IFAs in your area, access the FIND website (*www.find.co.uk*) and select IFAs from the 'Advice and information' section.

Managing your finances online

Paying bills online

Paying your bills through your online bank account is the same as transferring money from your account to another account. The way in which you do this will depend on your bank but in most cases it is a simple procedure of entering account and payment details. Some online banks provide help in the form of account and sort codes for a range of organisations that bill their customers, such as local authorities (council tax), and water, electricity and gas companies. In most cases regular payments are paid as standing orders or direct debits.

Getting a better deal

The Internet can help you find out if you are getting a good deal from your utility suppliers. With the recent deregulation, you have probably been inundated with service providers claiming to be able to cut your bills. From mobile phone charges through to gas and electricity, it seems that someone, somewhere can do it cheaper. The difficulty is knowing whether their claims are valid. Several websites have sprung up designed to help you find out whether you can, in fact, get a better deal elsewhere, and it is certainly worthwhile taking a look before changing supplier.

Switch with Which (*www.switchwithwhich.co.uk*) considers the service provided by energy suppliers and mobile phone companies, and directs you to sites that make a like-for-like comparison. *Which?* estimates that the average household could save up to £60 a year on its gas bill by changing to a rival company.

Money Net also provides a simple online questionnaire to help you determine whether you can save money on utilities (*www.moneynet.co.uk*). After analysing your responses the site will provide a list of alternative suppliers detailing how much you will save by swapping and stating any conditions that may apply. Alternatively, try Energy Watch (*www.energywatch.org.uk*) for advice and information on how to get the most from your utility provider as well as what to do if things go wrong.

You could also try Buy (*www.buy.co.uk*), the UK's first utilities price-comparison service, set up in 1998 with the aim of helping consumers find the cheapest energy suppliers in the deregulated market. The service now includes a range of other savings calculators, from phone bills to credit-card tariffs, to help you cut down on household bills.

For a full range of alternative sites use a search engine and search on the words 'utility comparison sites'.

State benefits and pensions

The site of the Department for Work and Pensions (*www.dwp.gov.uk*) provides information on benefits and pensions. It has four main sections for the general public: working age, pensions and retirement, families and children, and disabled people and carers. Each section contains information and also guides you to other relevant government sites.

Income tax

You can fill in and return your tax return online. The service has been available since April 2000 and has experienced some hiccups but in principle there are definite advantages to filling in your tax return electronically. The Inland Revenue's site (*www.inlandrevenue. gov.uk*) provides the option to use its software for this task or lists the commercial software that is acceptable. The software works out your tax bill for you and also helps to avoid omissions. Tax returns completed by hand are often returned to the sender because of missing information, so using the software is advantageous in that it will inform you of any missing details before the form is filed.

Summing up

To sum up, if you do decide to use financial sites bear in mind the following points.

- Compare the results from more than one site, and try out a few different sites.
- Some product-comparison sites are more comprehensive than others, and they sometimes have unique deals that aren't available anywhere else.
- Different product-comparison sites won't necessarily give you access to the same products.
- Read any terms and conditions, product details or the key features of financial products.
- Print off all relevant information and keep a copy.
- As soon as you receive paperwork or confirmation emails, check for mistakes and check through any documentation.
- Look for sites that have contact and customer support details on screen – these can be useful if you have any problems or questions.
- Think before you enter your email address into sites, as you may be bombarded with unsolicited emails.
- Sites that have advertising may be biased or not as independent as you think.

Chapter 13

Legal matters

Perhaps not surprisingly many people tend to shy away from handling their own legal matters, preferring instead to rely on the services of a professional lawyer to guide them through the minefield of complex procedures that lie at the heart of UK law. But even if at the end of the day you decide to go down the road of enlisting a lawyer of your own rather than attempting to deal with your affairs online, you can benefit substantially by using the Internet to do your groundwork.

At the very least, the Internet is a rich source of law-related information. Whatever your legal issue, there are Internet sites that will equip you with essential information and guide you towards asking focused questions when you do eventually consult a solicitor. It stands to reason that the more information you are able to gather yourself upfront, the less you will have to pay in legal bills in the long run. Given the hourly rates charged by most solicitors, investing one hour of your time in research can save you hundreds of pounds. And if you are willing to take the bull by the horns yourself, you can buy complete services via the Internet at a fraction of the cost of employing a solicitor.

As with many other aspects of getting an elife, there are numerous sites on tap and it can be difficult knowing just where to start. This chapter will introduce you to a selection of general law sites.

Useful fact-finding sites

Directories

As always, directory sites are a good place to start if you want to get an overview of just what is out there. For an excellent legal directory site try eLawOnline (*www.e-law-online.com*). There are a large number of links to legal websites spanning an assortment of categories. The site also contains current press articles relating to e-law.

Online guides

Interactive Law (*www.interactive-law.co.uk/*) describes itself as an online guide to UK law. The home page has sections for different areas of law such as property law, consumer law, Scottish law, criminal law and medical/clinical negligence law, although you may find that when you click on some links the outlines of the law appear to be quite scant. The site is particularly useful as a vehicle for pointing you towards a solicitor in your postcode area.

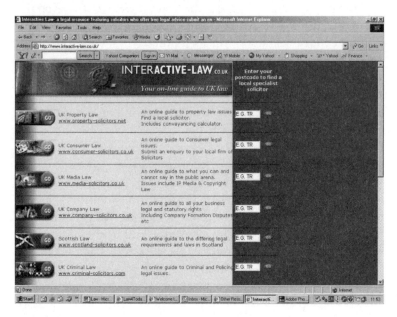

Each category is linked to a specialist site relating to the area that you have selected. 'UK medical/clinical negligence law', for instance, links to *www.medical-accidents.co.uk/*. The latter site gives very brief coverage of the area in question, giving an explanation of what is meant by negligence, outlining the procedures for making a claim, providing a search facility so that you can locate a solicitor in your area who is competent to deal with this aspect of the law as well as giving you an idea of the duration and cost that may be involved in making a case.

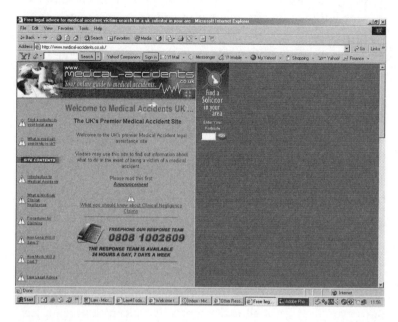

For a clear idea of your rights to do with booking holidays online, visit the zone called 'Your law' at *www.law4today.com* and read the 'Travel' section. The site itself provides a down-to-earth and some-times humorous approach to law and stacks of useful information that can help you deal with run-of-the mill legal issues. The Travel section explains your rights relating to different types of holidays such as package holidays, organised tours and scheduled flights. It outlines the kind of contract that you would normally enter into and explains in simple terms what this means to you, the traveller. For example, if you have booked a holiday with a tour operator through a travel agent, then it is likely that your contract is with the tour operator and not the travel agent. The tour operator will be responsible for all aspects of your holiday including your accom-modation, pre-arranged car hire and transport. The travel agent will be responsible for making sure that the administrative side of the booking runs smoothly. The site also provides lots of useful tips that can help protect your interests and prevent things going wrong in the first place.

Portals

Some sites are referred to as one-stop shops or portals because they provide information or services over and above that which can be expected from a typical website. In the area of law this may mean the inclusion of interesting legal news items, outcomes of particular cases or changes to the current law. eLawOnline recommends a good site that it classes as a UK portal. It is maintained by Delia Venables and can be found at *www.venables.co.uk/*. The site is easy to navigate, with information designed for individuals, companies, students and lawyers. It is also well-respected and is widely used by lawyers. You can search for free legal information by topic area such as family matters, human rights, immigration, harassment and crime, to name but a few. Each category is also accompanied by an extensive network of links to other sites that provide further information or services in that area.

LAW on the Web (*www.lawontheweb.co.uk/intro.htm*) has received several commendations for its content, including one from the BBC, which declared it to be 'one of the UK's best online legal resources'. The site is very well produced and provides clear, no-nonsense coverage of all major topics. It contains a page on legal news that covers a medley of legal headlines taken from a cross-section of newspapers. There is also an area that lists solicitors who have experience of dealing with law outside the UK – particularly useful if you are buying a property abroad.

Buying legal services

Legal issues are rarely straightforward, and individual circumstances can create a significant variation among cases of the same nature. Perhaps because of this, most legal services on the Net are offered as part of a hybrid solution and you will usually have the opportunity to pick and choose the right combination for you. These services generally include:

- being able to download legal documents and forms from the Internet
- the facility to browse a large database of law-related information
- the option to have questions and answers delivered via email
- the choice to speak to or visit a solicitor by phone or in person.

Case history

Andrea is a single parent with two young children, one of whom suffers periodically from serious asthma attacks. Andrea's ex-partner sees the children only every few months. As they never married, Andrea was concerned that should the children need medical attention while they were with their father, he would not be able to give his consent to treatment. Before paying for a solicitor Andrea decided to look at a few legal websites to see if this was a common problem. She says, ' I came across a site that had a question from someone in a very similar situation to my own. I found out that I could make a parental responsibility agreement with my ex-partner which would then give him the legal right to be involved in the health, education and welfare of our children. In my case, it also meant that should Toby need urgent treatment for his asthma, my ex-partner would be able to sign a medical consent form.'

Documents

There are lots of sites that offer ready-made and even tailored legal documents that you can purchase online. Try Compact Law, one of the UK's leading law portals. From its site (*www.compactlaw.co.uk/*) you can search for free legal information on key topics such as adoption or housing. You can also purchase legal documents that best fit your needs. For example, if you are looking to prepare a will then this site can help you locate just the right will for you. There are wills that are suitable for married females without children, wills that take into account the needs of single parents and so on.

Also try Desktop Lawyer (*www.desktoplawyer.co.uk/dt/browse/law/*). After you decide on the type of document you need, a software program will guide you through the process of completing the form online by asking you questions relating to your personal circumstances.

The government Court Service website (*www.courtservice.gov.uk*) has all the court forms available to download and helpful information leaflets designed for the public.

A personal service

You can also go one step further and engage the services of a solicitor on a fixed-task, fixed-fee basis. Legalservicesshop.com (*www.freelawyer.co.uk/about_us.htm*) runs what it terms a Legal Services Shop. In addition to providing free access to a database of legal information, it also makes available a pre-determined legal service for a fixed charge. For example, at the time of writing, a solicitor will draft a document to change your name by deed poll for £45 or carry out an uncontested divorce for £425 (both inclusive of VAT), providing that you and your spouse have agreed to divorce and have no outstanding financial or custodial issues. In the event of your situation being more complicated, the legal services shop will try to match you with an appropriately qualified solicitor in your vicinity and quote you on an hourly basis for this work. However, as always, before you decide to go ahead try a range of sites and compare the value of the services on offer.

Finding a solicitor

If at the outset you decide to go down the road of finding a solicitor to act on your behalf rather than attempting a DIY job online, then the Law Society's site Solicitors Online (*www.solicitors-online.com*) is a good place to start. The Law Society is the regulatory body for the legal profession, responsible for establishing and monitoring competency standards among its members. It has records of all law firms or individual solicitors that come under its jurisdiction throughout England and Wales. You can search its records free of charge. This site provides a service of the Law Society for England and Wales. For other parts of the UK, contact the Law Society for Northern Ireland (*www.lawsoc-ni.org*) and the Law Society for Scotland (*www.lawscot.org.uk*).

If a solicitor is featured in the database as having a specialism, you can be assured that his or her skills have been assessed and affirmed by the Law Society. The database is updated each day and includes specialist categories such as family law, immigration, medical negligence, personal injury, insolvency licensed practitioners and criminal litigation. The site is an invaluable source of information.

The Law Society is not the only site that has an online database of solicitors. You can also search the Online Law database (*www.online-law.co.uk/*), free of charge. This will help you to find firms of solicitors in England and Wales (although not individual solicitors). You can also get a list of courts in England and Wales.

One of the most helpful sites about sources of legal advice of all kinds is that of the Community Legal Service (CLS, *www.justask. org.uk*). This lists solicitors and other advice organisations across the country by area. Agencies listed must have achieved the quality mark of the CLS.

Public funding

Public funding is the new term for what used to be called 'legal aid'. It is administered by the Legal Services Commission. Its website (*www.legalservices.gov.uk*) has a wealth of information about public funding including all the information leaflets for the general public. You can find out whether you would be eligible for public funding and the areas of work that it covers.

Finding out about your rights

There are lots of useful sites that you can visit to find out about your legal rights. Here are a few that you might like to try.

For your rights as a consumer try the Office of Fair Trading (*www.oft.gov.uk*) and the Citizens Advice Bureau (*www.adviceguide. org.uk*). For your rights as an employee try the Department of Trade and Industry (*www.dti.gov.uk*) and Tailored Interactive Guidance on Employment Rights (*www.tiger.gov.uk*). If you want to know your rights as a taxpayer visit *www.inlandrevenue.gov.uk*. If you need information on going to court try the Court Service for England and Wales (*www.courtservice.gov.uk*), the Court Service for Scotland (*www.scotcourts.gov.uk*) or the Court Service for Northern Ireland (*www.northernireland.gov.uk/pubsec/courts/*).

Chapter 14

Entertainment and leisure

The Internet has many practical uses but a whole range of websites has been designed purely to help you to enjoy your leisure time. Whether it involves checking out the sports results, booking tickets for the theatre or playing online bingo, the Internet has the resources to bring you the most up-to-date information, features and games.

The number of sites dedicated to leisure pursuits is vast, and this chapter introduces you to a few of them.

Sport

Whether you play or just watch sport, you will be spoilt for choice when it comes to sports websites. The Internet is the perfect medium for bringing you up-to-date sporting news, reviews and results, with web pages being continuously updated.

For in-depth, all-round sports coverage you cannot beat the BBC's sporting section (*www.bbc.co.uk/sport*). The home page will keep you updated with breaking news and topical articles, as well as providing a sporting calendar and links to pages dedicated to specific sports. One of the site's major appeals has to be the excellent video and audio coverage taken from BBC television and radio (see *Online TV and radio*, below). Alternatively, try the Sportal website (*www.sportal.com*). As the name suggests, Sportal is a portal site providing a one-stop shop for all the latest sporting news and reviews. UK Sport (*www.uksport.gov.uk*) is another excellent site for impartial news and topical articles from the world of sport.

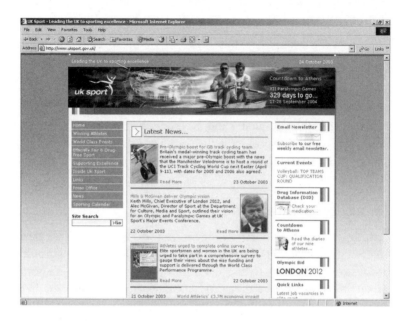

Fantasy sports

In fantasy sports the idea is to create your own team, based on a budget and then monitor its progress through the season. The fantasy team comprises 'real' players from different teams or leagues. For example, in fantasy football you create a dream team by buying players from any of the teams in the league within a specified budget. If the players in your team actually score a goal in their (real) league matches then that goal can be credited to your fantasy team.

If you are new to fantasy sport try the BBC's fantasy football league (*http://bbcfootball.fantasyleague.co.uk/*). This is a monthly game and it is free to play. You have £50m to spend on 11 players, and how you spend it is entirely up to you. Once you have picked your side, the next task is to make sure that the team keeps scoring points. You also have six transfers available during each Game Month, so if one of your players isn't performing well you can bring in a fresh face.

If you get the taste for fantasy sport you can then move on to one of the sites hosted by the major players in this area. Fantasy League is a popular site (*www.fantasyleague.com*) providing games for football, golf and Formula 1 racing. It serves over 300,000 Fantasy League teams in the UK via its web servers, telephone lines and phone operators. The company that set it up estimates that there are now almost a million people playing Fantasy League's licensed games worldwide. Alternatively, have a look at Dream League (*www.dreamleague.com*), which concentrates on football, cricket and motor sport.

There are online games for numerous other sports including cycling, cricket, horse-racing and even handball. To find a site specialising in a specific sport, type the search words 'fantasy sport' followed by the name of the sport in the search box of your favourite search engine.

Tickets for sports events

Getting tickets for sports events is notoriously difficult, often involving queuing in the cold for hours on end or spending hours trying to get through to the ticket hotline by telephone. Before subjecting yourself to either ordeal it is worth checking whether you can buy tickets online. You will find that many (but not all) of the sport websites provide options to buy tickets online. In addition to sports-specific sites, general ticket-finder websites also cater for sports events. Sites such as *www.londonticketshop.co.uk* and *www.ticket-finders.com* provide categories for sporting events and usually include both UK and international fixtures.

Football

If football is your passion you will find plenty to keep you entertained. TeamTalk (*www.teamtalk.com*) is one of the oldest and most respected football websites providing general information from the British leagues as well as international clubs. Or you could try the Football Association's site (*www.the-fa.org*). With a section on women's football as well as a kid's page, this site attempts to include all the family.

If you like to keep up to date on football statistics, try *www.soccer-stats.com* – it contains all the statistics you could ever want. Soccer Net (*www.soccernet.com*) is another comprehensive site providing statistics, league tables and topical new items.

You will also find that the majority of teams have their own websites providing details of fixtures, results, news and gossip. If the website address is not obvious try using a popular search engine to search for the club's name.

If your team is playing away, take a look at the Football Ground Guide website (*www.footballgroundguide.co.uk*). This site is packed with facts for away supporters with photographs of the grounds, directions, and even advice on where to go for a pint before the game.

Formula 1 racing

If you are a fan of motor sports, the BBC's site is an excellent place to start (*www.bbc.co.uk/f1*). There is plenty of general information as well as specialist features such as 'Inside the cars', where you can see how the parts of the car work and fit together. The site also provides an analysis of all the teams and a profile for each driver. F1 enthusiasts will love the circuit guide, which takes you around every F1 circuit with audio accompaniment and speedometer readings to show you exactly how to take those bends.

Horse-racing

The Cheltenham site (*www.cheltenham.co.uk*) is fairly representative of a racecourse website, providing details of fixtures, a site plan as well as details of hospitality and sponsorship opportunities. There is also an option to buy tickets online.

For racing in Scotland, try *www.scottishracing.co.uk*. This site covers the five Scottish racecourses and gives details of forthcoming meetings, news and links to other relevant sites.

For further related sites search on the words 'horse-racing' using your favourite search engine. You will find that the majority of sites specialise in online betting and statistics. For further information on betting online see *Gambling online* later in this chapter.

Tennis

For news and reviews try *www.tennis.com* or *www.guardian.co.uk/sport* and choose the tennis option from the menu. Both sites will keep you abreast of developments from around the world.

Tennis fans will find plenty to keep them occupied at the Wimbledon site (*www.wimbledon.org*). There is a virtual tour of the grounds, video clips from classic matches as well as information on how to enter the ballot for a ticket for the next tournament.

For those who play tennis or would like to learn, *www.tennisland. co.uk* provides details of clubs around the UK as well as details of coaches for those needing to refine their technique.

Cricket

Cricket 365 (*www.cricket365.com*) provides features such as live coverage of matches, fixture information, reports and previews as well as links to sites specialising in other popular sports. There is also a direct link to the cricket pages of the auction site eBay where you can pick up new or second-hand cricket equipment (see Chapter 7 information on auction websites).

For all the latest news and scores try *www.ecb.co.uk*, promoted as the official home of English cricket on the Internet. Alternatively, visit the sports section of the BBC site (*www.bbc.co.uk/sport*) and select the 'Cricket' option from the menu. If you support county cricket you will find that the majority of clubs also have their own websites. If the site name is not obvious, use a search engine to track it down.

Other sports

There are plenty of other sports to choose from. To find a site dedicated to a specific sport type the name of the sport in the search box of your favourite search engine. Unless your interest lies with a minority sport you should find that you are spoilt for choice.

Last, but not least, if you are an armchair (or pub stool) sports fanatic try the Sports Pubs site (*www.sportspubs.co.uk*). This site provides a list of all the best venues in which to watch televised sports. It also tells you which pubs to frequent if you support specific countries.

Theatre

If you enjoy the performing arts the Internet can provide details of performance times, prices and availability of tickets. On many sites you can also book your tickets online, thereby bypassing the queues and preventing the disappointment of a sold-out performance.

Finding out what's on

The first step is to find out what is currently playing at venues in your locality. UK Theatre on the Web (*www.uktw.co.uk*) provides details of both professional and amateur theatre, dance and opera UK-wide. The site has a search option where you select the type of entertainment and then enter either the name of the performance, or your town or region. The site will provide details on the selected performance or a list of all current productions in the region specified.

Alternatively, try the What's on Stage website (*www.whatsonstage. com*). This site describes itself as the UK's biggest and best online guide to the performing arts. At any one time, its database can contain information on more than 2,500 performances around the country including theatre, opera, classical music, dance, ballet, comedy and pantomime. If you want to go out in London, the London Theatre site (*www.londontheatre.co.uk*) provides details for performances.

When it comes to Christmas time, try *www.its-behind-you.com* for specific information on pantomimes.

Buying tickets online

The majority of sites mentioned in the previous section, and most ticket agents, also provide an option to buy tickets online. Booking fees can vary substantially, so it is worth shopping around and comparing rates. Also, when buying via an agency, make sure you know the face value of the ticket you're buying. If an agency cannot confirm the price, don't buy the ticket as you have no way of telling how good a seat you are getting.

Case history

Maggie was organising a weekend for some friends in London and had been set the task of finding a musical show for the Saturday afternoon. Armed with a few website addresses she decided to compare availability and price.

'I started with a general ticket-finding site, *www.ticket-finders. com*, and selected the 'Theatre' option. After selecting 'London' as the city and 'Musicals' as the type of theatre, I was presented with a choice of performances. I decided to look at *Bombay Dreams* at the Apollo theatre. There was only one price quoted, and it was a little steep so I decided to check out some more sites before booking.

'I then looked at the UK Theatre World site (*www.uktw.co.uk*). I clicked on the 'Tickets' option and then scrolled down the list of performances until I found *Bombay Dreams*. Tickets from this site were quoted as costing £14 to £40 but when I selected the date of the performance the only tickets available were priced at £40 or £45, and there was a £6.75 processing fee to be added to the price of each ticket. I had the taste for it now so I also checked out *www.whatsonstage.com*. Again, tickets were quoted as costing £14 to £40 and when I went through to the booking screen it looked just the same as the previous site and the prices were exactly the same.

'My last try was *www.londontheatre.co.uk*. I found this site extremely confusing. It was fine for information but when it came to trying to buy a ticket it seemed to be offering tickets for only one performance and it wasn't *Bombay Dreams*, so I gave up. Back to the UK Theatre World site and I booked four tickets at £40 each (plus the booking fee) for our weekend in June.'

Tip

Before you purchase tickets online make sure that the site has a security policy. For further information see Chapter 7.

Cinema

Cinemas Online (*www.cinemas-online.co.uk*) provides details of cinema show times UK-wide. Simply select your region of the UK and scroll through the listings until you find your town. Alternatively, you can access the cinema websites direct. Use *www.yell.com* to search for cinemas in your town and click on the website link.

Film buffs should try the British Film Institute's website (*www.bfi.org.uk*). As well as news and reviews this site also provides the Film Links Gateway, a facility intended to provide a wide-reaching but selective collection of websites relating to film and the media.

Museums and galleries

The Museums website (*www.museums.co.uk*) provides information on museums and galleries throughout the UK. You start by searching on a town or postcode and then specify a distance from that initial start point. So, for example, if you search on Leeds and specify a 15-mile search area, you are presented with choices for museums and galleries in Leeds, Bradford and Wakefield. As well as providing

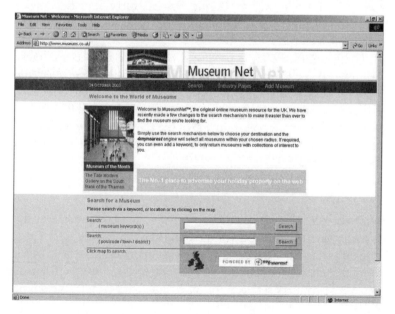

the address and telephone number it also has links to museums that have their own websites.

For national sites try National Museums of Scotland (*www.nms. ac.uk*) or National Museums and Galleries of Wales (*www.nmgw. ac.uk*). For London attractions, access the Visit London site (*www. visitlondon.com*) and search for museums.

Hobbies and interests

The range of hobbies and interests pursued by people in the UK is so large and diverse that this section can act only as an introduction to some of the more popular ones. If you have a specific interest you can easily find related sites by searching on the name of the hobby using any popular search engine. If you are looking to join a club or group that meets locally, also include your town or region in the search box.

Collecting

The Internet opens up a whole new world to collectors. Not only can you source additions to your collection locally, you can now make contact with collectors around the world. There are sites dedicated to all kinds of items that people collect: for example, you can add to your collection of Beanie Babies (furry toys filled with beans) by visiting *www.beaniebonkers.co.uk*, or of stamps by going to *www.stamplink.com*.

The auction site eBay (*www.ebay.co.uk*) is a good source for tracking down that elusive missing piece for your collection. Select the 'Collectibles' option from the menu. The resulting list of options is substantial and your requirement is more than likely to be included. If not, use the search box at the top of the screen to carry out a thorough search of the site. For further details on auction sites take a look at Chapter 7.

Photography

With the introduction of digital cameras, the computer and the Internet have become tools of the trade in photography.

Companies involved in developing photographs have been quick to offer their services online. To encourage you to try them, many also offer periphery services, free of charge. For example, the online photo developer, Fotango (*www.fotango.com*), provides a free download to help you organise your photographs and create online photograph albums.

Photofun (*www.photofun.com*) is another site that will help you make the most of your digital photographs. You can create your own website, make a scrapbook, set up a slideshow with music or send e-cards. This versatile site is easy to navigate and a must if you need to organise your growing number of digital photos.

Puzzles and games

The All Jigsaw Puzzles website (*www.alljigsawpuzzles.co.uk*) claims to be the UK's leading online jigsaw puzzle store. With over 350 'hard to find' jigsaws available to buy online, this site has puzzles that range from 5 to 18,000 pieces.

If you would rather do your jigsaw on the computer, try the puzzles from Shockwave (*www.shockwave.com*) from Macromedia. This is a fascinating site that will keep you occupied for hours. You can choose from the selected puzzles or you can create your own from a photograph, all for free.

If you enjoy crosswords take a look at *www.crossword-puzzles.co.uk*. This site has a crossword compiler so that you can create your own crossword, as well as a wide range of interactive crosswords to complete online. The site also has links to other sites that provide software, books, dictionaries and crossword-solving products.

Computer games

The Internet provides the opportunity to play plenty of computer games, mostly free. Some websites include free games simply to attract visitors to their site. Others use advertising to provide revenue. To track down free games type the words 'computer games free' in the search box of a search engine. You will probably come across a site aptly named Play Free Online Games (*www.playfreeonlinegames.co.uk*) as well as a host of others.

Gambling online

The global betting and gaming market is estimated at being worth $1 trillion, with the online industry contributing an increasing proportion of this revenue.

Gambling online is a popular leisure pursuit. A recent survey by BT Openworld found that over 24 per cent of the men interviewed had placed an online bet within the last year. This contrasted sharply with the women surveyed: none of them had used online betting facilities.

Sports betting

If you like a flutter on the horses or a bet on your football team you will find the Sporting Life website (*www.sportinglife.com*) a good source of information. The site is affiliated to the racing newspaper of the same name and claims to combine the benefits of the Internet (immediacy and innovation) with the reputation of the newspaper for authority. This site also includes online betting options, as does its sister site, *www.bettingzone.co.uk*. Betting Zone also specialises in providing independent betting news, previews, analysis and statistics. Alternatively, try *www.sportingodds.com*.

If you prefer to stick with your favourite high street betting shop you will find that the majority have an online presence. William Hill (*www.willhill.com*) and Ladbrokes (*www.ladbrokes.com*) are just two examples of businesses that have successfully captured the online market.

Casino gambling and games

The Internet has thousands of gambling sites, many of which are bright, noisy and extremely busy with advertising slogans popping up every few seconds. Your best route to finding a good site is personal recommendation. Alternatively, the Casino Choice (*www.casinochoice.co.uk*) website, which specifically reviews UK sites, may be a good place to start.

If you enjoy a game of bingo give it a try online. The Free Online Bingo site (*www.freeonlinebingo.com*) provides links to plenty of sites that host bingo games. If you prefer the atmosphere at a live venue you can locate your nearest Gala Bingo club and register for free membership online by accessing its site at *www.gala-bingo.co.uk*.

The Internet can also keep you up to date with the National Lottery. If you miss the draw, you can always check the lottery results at *www.national-lottery.co.uk*.

Music

Whatever your musical taste the Internet will be able to provide details of concerts, news and reviews as well as enabling you to purchase CDs and download music directly to your PC. A good starting point is the directory site Top 10 Sites (*www.top10sites.net*). If you cannot find your favourite artist from within the categories try searching for his or her website by typing the name into the search box of a search engine.

Downloading music

The Internet has had a huge impact on the music industry. Music files can easily be downloaded from the Internet, allowing you to sample tracks before buying a CD – you can even download the entire CD to your PC.

Music is downloaded as MP3 files, the industry standard for music stored in a digital format. MP3 files can be stored on your computer or copied on to recordable CDs. If you want to play an MP3 file through you computer you will need to have speakers and a soundcard as well as a special software plug-in known as a media player that allows you to listen to music. The latest web browsers have these already built in. Internet Explorer includes Windows Media Player and Netscape has Winamp. Other popular products are RealPlayer (*www.real.com*), which is suitable for both the PC and Mac, and Quicken (*www.apple.com/quicktime*) for the Mac.

The one drawback to downloading music is the time it takes. If you have broadband it may not be an issue, but depending on the speed of your modem it can be a slow process, with a three-minute track taking up to ten minutes to load with a 56Kbps modem and up to 20 minutes with a 28.8Kbps modem.

Downloading music has become a controversial subject because of copyright issues. A well-known site, Napster (*www.napster.com*), was closed down owing to infringement of copyright. Napster is an extremely popular digital-music-sharing service, but until issues can be resolved with the record companies it is unlikely to reopen for business.

Festivals and gigs

Bigmouth (*www.bigmouth.co.uk*) is the perfect site for anyone who likes to be up to date on general music news and gossip. The site provides listings of tours and gigs throughout the UK as well as a free subscription service that sends an email to all members detailing forthcoming events. The site also has a useful A to Z of artists, with links to the relevant group's or singer's website. For further information on music festivals try the E-Festivals site (*www. efestivals.co.uk*). As well as keeping you informed of forthcoming festivals and gigs, this site also has a community section with a chatroom and discussion forums.

The Classical Music site (*www.classicalmusic.co.uk*) provides concert listings, articles, news and features. If you enjoy music in the fresh air, keep your eye on the Picnic Concerts website (*www. picnicconcerts.com*) for up-to-date listings of outdoor concerts.

Buying CDs online

Buying online has to be one of the cheapest ways of acquiring CDs. At the time of writing, most current chart CDs could be found for £8.99 including delivery. The high street outlets cannot compete with this discounted price. CD Wow (*www.cd-wow.com*) seems to keep prices down by importing CDs from Hong Kong. This does not impact on the purchaser as postage is free and, in case you are concerned, the CDs are originals, not pirated copies. It is also worth trying Amazon

(*www.amazon.co.uk*) and Play 247 (*www.play247.com*) – both sites also have some good deals.

If you are a jazz fan and find it difficult to track down CDs from the high street music shops, try the Jazz CD website (www.jazzcd.co.uk). As well as a shopping section this site also provides music reviews and links to other related sites.

Online TV and radio

Our home computers are slowly but surely becoming transformed into all-singing, all-dancing entertainment centres. You can watch DVDs, download your favourite music, play a standard CD, listen to live radio and even watch TV.

Internet radio

Internet radio provides far more choice and variety than conventional radio. If you want to listen online your computer will need to have speakers and a soundcard as well as a media player.

Your web browser will usually have a media player built in but you may find that you also need to install additional players (see *Downloading music*, above). For instance, the majority of the BBC's audio and video clips need RealPlayer. If you try to play a clip that is not supported by your media player you are likely to be prompted to download the required player. Simply select the 'OK' option and you are all set. There is no need to worry that you will overwrite your original player as you can have as many different media players loaded as you need.

The majority of the major radio stations have an option to link to their scheduled programmes online. If you want to give it a try, take a look at the BBC's online radio webpage (*www.bbc.co.uk/radio*). Alternatively, try Virgin radio (*www.virginradio.co.uk*).

There are also thousands of radio stations that have only an online presence. Unlike traditional radio stations, many of these sites have continuous music without the standard interruptions from the DJ or the adverts from commercial stations. With some stations you can also take control and skip tracks that you do not like. For a full range of online radio stations type the words 'online radio' into the search box of your favourite search engine or use the Radio Locator search engine (*www.radio-locator.com*).

> **Tip**
>
> If you are using Internet Explorer, you can access a huge range of online radio stations by accessing the 'View' menu and selecting the 'Toolbar' option. Click the 'Radio stations' button on the toolbar and select 'Radio stations, radio station guide'.

Internet TV

Making Internet TV work is far more difficult than listening to the radio online. With a modem connection to the Internet streamed video is almost always jerky and playable only in a small window. Realistically, you need to have a broadband connection to even contemplate paying for a video service, but if you have a modem connection it is still worth taking a look at video clips that are free of charge. Many news, sports and entertainment sites include video links with the option to compress the stream for dial-up connections. This does reduce the quality of the picture but it is still worth trying.

At the moment, the Internet is no substitute for TV but it has found a niche accompanying some TV productions. During the Channel 4 Big Brother series, live action was streamed from the reality TV house via the Internet. It is claimed that 7 million viewers accessed the site following one particular episode.

Unfortunately, watching TV on your computer does not negate the need to purchase a TV licence, but your standard TV licence does also cover your PC.

For further information on Internet TV and radio, see the report in *Computing Which?* (March 2003), which you can access on Which? Online (*www.which.net*).

Chapter 15

Health

Health warning

There is no doubt that the Internet is an excellent source for health information, but whether it is also a useful place to consult with a doctor or buy medicines is another matter. According to a report in *Health Which?* (June 2000), you should think again if you are tempted to buy prescription drugs or health advice over the Internet. Research found that the advice given was sometimes poor, and occasionally even dangerous.

The Internet is brimming with health-related information: thousands of sites specialise in health, with many offering online medical consultations and therapy sessions and even selling prescription drugs online. Although it may be convenient to access, the advice can prove to be inaccurate and, unfortunately, you cannot rely on legislation to protect you from misleading health information on the Internet. So this is one area of the Internet where you should exercise extreme caution. Plenty of excellent sites do exist, providing clear and accurate information, but you have to be very careful to stick to impartial sites hosted by well-known establishments and take heed of the guidelines in this chapter.

Searching for information

Health and educational websites are popular destinations on the Internet. But with such a vast amount of information on the Net, it can be difficult to track down specific facts. Unless you have had a site recommended to you, a search engine is usually the best place to start, particularly if you learn how to search selectively (see Chapter 2). By simply entering a symptom or a category of disease (such as cancer) you are likely to bring up a list of thousands of sites. You can limit this list by narrowing your search to include only UK websites or by specifying a more specific search phrase, such as oral cancer. In both cases the list of possible sites should be more manageable.

Reliability of information

Once you have found a site, how can you be sure that the information is up to date and reliable? By its very nature, information on the Internet can be kept bang up to date. Make sure that the site you choose regularly updates information (there should be a last updated entry somewhere on the home page) and that there are references to topical news items.

As for reliability, you have to bear in mind that information can be put on the Internet by absolutely anyone and that you must not believe everything you read. It is certainly worth keeping a degree of scepticism and verifying your findings with another site or two. To maximise your chances of finding accurate information stick to academic sites and those managed by reputable organisations such as independent and well-known charities.

Once you have found a site that you like the look of, use these simple checks to establish whether the information can be trusted.

- Where does the information come from? Is the source qualified to provide this type of information? Generally, authoritative sources, such as medical libraries, universities, government bodies and charities, are reliable. However, just being hosted by a reputable source doesn't guarantee its content, so check carefully who the articles are written by.
- Is the site providing facts or opinions? If it is a commercial site, is the information biased? Approach websites produced by commercial sites with some caution. If you are not sure if a site is commercial, email it to find out.
- Does the site make it clear who the information is aimed at?
- When was the site last updated?
- Are there adequate references to show where the content comes from? Is the content clearly attributed?

Which? and *Health Which?* both review health-related sites regularly and recommend reliable ones. Visit Which? Online (*www.which.net*) to access the latest articles – this is free for subscribers to Which? Online; if you are not a subscriber you could sign up for a free trial.

Health directories

If you still have concerns about the quality of the sites you have visited, try using a health directory as a means of finding a reputable site. A health directory provides an index of links to health-related sites, narrowing your search and saving you time. As a bonus, some directories also assess the content of a site so that only reputable sites are included. Some directory sites such as Health on the Net (*www.hon.ch*) provide a full range of links and also specify whether a site meets a pre-defined code of conduct. Produced by a non-profit-making foundation based in Geneva, Heath on the Net provides a gateway to a full range of international sites. There is an option on the home page to select 'Patients and individuals' or 'Medical professionals'. This ensures that the search will return information appropriate for the audience. When 'asthma' was entered in the search box, the site returned 4,259 results, 182 of which were flagged as being on sites subscribing to the HON code of practice. The HON code includes the following requirements:

- only medically trained and qualified professionals will give advice unless clearly stated as otherwise
- the information provided is designed to support – not replace – the patient–doctor relationship
- confidentiality and privacy will honour or exceed legal requirements
- clear references will be provided to the source of data.

Healthfinder (*www.healthfinder.gov*) is a US directory specifically designed for consumers. It has a search facility and provides health news and information. This site returned 60 references when searching for information on asthma. For a UK bias try Organising Medical Networked Information (OMNI) from Nottingham University (*www.omni.ac.uk*). This site markets itself as the UK's gateway to high-quality Internet resources for health and medicine. It is well-designed and easy to use. In order to assure the quality of information, experts are employed to identify credible sites. When searching for information on asthma, 108 results were returned.

The National Electronic Library For Health (*www.nelh.nhs.uk*) is another excellent resource.

Health sites

The range of health sites available on the Internet is ever-increasing. You can find sites that specialise in different areas of health, or you can try more general sites providing a full range of advice and information on health-related issues.

General health sites

For advice on consumer issues to do with health, consult Which? Online (*www.which.net*), looking particularly for articles in *Health Which?*.

Another site worth a look is *www.bbc.co.uk/health*, the BBC's offering. This site provides a full range of health-related information including articles on topical issues. If you are looking for information on health legislation, try *www.who.dk*, the World Health Organisation's site. This site has a more formal feel than the two above, but it has an excellent directory of health topics. The Department of Health's website (*www.doh.gov.uk*) is another useful site.

Sites for specific health conditions

Many people turn to the Internet in search of specific medical information. If an illness or condition has been diagnosed it is often difficult to take in all the information presented by the doctor or consultant. It can be helpful to do your own research and find out as much as you can about the condition.

Other sites you may like to try for information on cancer include Cancerbacup (*www.cancerbacup.org.uk*), Cancer Research UK (*www.cancerhelp.org.uk*) and the Macmillan CancerLine (*www.macmillan.org.uk*).

If you require information on heart conditions, the British Heart Foundation's site (*www.bhf.org.uk*) is a good starting point. It provides help on improving your lifestyle and combating heart disease. The

---

Case history

When Laura found that she had breast cancer, after the initial shock and disbelief, she wanted to find out everything she could about the condition.

'A friend showed me a recent copy of *Health Which?* (December 2002). There was an article on breast cancer that included a list of sites that provided quality information on breast cancer.

'I tried three sites. The Royal Marsden Hospital's patient information website (*www.royalmarsden.org/patientinfo/booklets/breast_cancer/index.asp*) helped answer many of my initial questions about the disease. Breast Cancer Care (*www.breastcancercare.org.uk*) gave me useful practical information. I also found the personal accounts by people affected by cancer very helpful. On the third site I visited, *www.dipex.org*, I read about people's experiences of serious illness.

'I found all three sites really helpful. I was able to understand my condition and it gave me the confidence to ask questions when I saw my own doctor. I would certainly recommend using the Internet to find out about an illness. It certainly gave me some strength during a very tough time.'

Association for Children with Heart Disorders (*www.tachd.org.uk*) is a registered charity providing specific advice for children with heart conditions.

In general, if you are looking for specific information, use a search engine and type appropriate keywords in the search box. It is advisable to select sites that are familiar to you or sites that are hosted by academic or charitable organisations.

Complementary medicine

The range of complementary healthcare services available in the UK increases on an almost daily basis. For information on the Internet pertaining to complementary therapies start by visiting the sites of the umbrella organisations representing complementary medicine in the UK. Examples include the British Complementary Medicine

Association (*www.bcma.co.uk*) and the Institute for Complementary Medicine (*www.icmedicine.co.uk*). Both of them represent practitioners of various therapies, and have links to the professional bodies of individual therapies. *The Which? Guide to Complementary Therapies* provides detailed information and website addresses for reputable organisations.

The NHS online

The National Health Service's website can be found at *www.nhs.uk*. This site bills itself as the official gateway to National Health Service organisations on the Internet. It connects you to your local NHS services and provides national information about the NHS: what it does, how it works and how to use it. The home page provides useful options to find out how your local hospitals are performing and just how long you are likely to have to wait for a hospital appointment.

The NHS site also provides a direct link to the NHS Direct website. NHS Direct is a telephone helpline available 24 hours a day. Designed to make the NHS more accessible, this helpline is manned by qualified nursing staff trained to answer medical queries. The service is complemented by an online Internet service, NHS Direct Online (*www.nhsdirect.nhs.uk*). This site provides general health information and lifestyle advice. There are sections tackling topical health issues as well as an online medical encyclopaedia.

If you or a member of your family have specific symptoms, access the 'Self-help guide' option. Read the information and then click on the 'Body key' option. To get started you select the part of the body that is causing the major discomfort. You will then be guided through a series of questions relating to your symptoms. Your responses will result in the system directing you to one of three options. You will be advised to manage the problem yourself, call NHS Direct or telephone 999 for emergency assistance. Although none of the options advises you to contact your GP, the NHS Direct telephone service will suggest this option if appropriate.

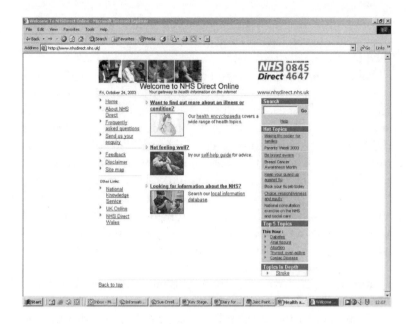

Private health consultations online

There are a growing number of health sites that specialise in providing online consultations ranging from counselling through to diagnosing medical conditions.

Safety and quality issues

Online health consultations can most certainly be convenient but are they safe? You may bypass the queue for an appointment and avoid the busy waiting rooms but will you receive advice that is medically sound?

This very much depends on the person handing out the advice. The most obvious concern when considering an online consultation is the experience and qualifications of the person responding to your query. Unfortunately, many sites do not even name their consultants let alone provide details of qualifications and legal registration.

If you are using a UK-based medical site the doctors should be regulated by the General Medical Council (GMC). As long as the site names its doctors you can check on their credentials by visiting the GMC site (*www.gmc-uk.org*). If you are using a site based in a

253

country other than the UK, the doctors will not be registered with the GMC and you have no way of knowing whether they are qualified to offer medical advice.

Your legal position depends on where the site is located. If you use a UK site that provides the services of UK-registered doctors, you have the legal right to expect the service to be provided with 'reasonable care and skill'. If this is found not to be the case, you have the right to seek compensation, even if the site contains a waiver to exclude such liability (UK sites should not include this type of waiver as they are not legally binding and will not stand up in court).

Sites outside of the UK are quite a different story. The same consumer protection laws do not cover foreign sites and you may find you have no comeback if you receive poor or even dangerous advice. You will find that some US sites include extensive waivers of liability, doing little to instil confidence.

You may also have concerns regarding patient confidentiality. Most sites do provide assurance that their sites are safe but it is difficult to assess if the safeguards are sufficient. Check that the site does have a policy and then read the small print. Make sure that you are happy with the steps the site takes to ensure privacy and confidentiality before you sign up.

Buying medicines online

In Europe it is illegal for manufacturers of medicines to advertise prescription drugs directly to the public. But in the USA this is far from the case: the sale of drugs is a billion-dollar industry. With access to American websites from anywhere in the world there is nothing to stop someone from outside the USA purchasing prescription drugs.

Once you have tracked down a site offering this service, buying drugs over the Internet is a relatively simple task. In most cases you are required to complete a medical questionnaire online, specify the quantity of the drug you require and provide your credit-card details. Most sites claim that your questionnaire is then thoroughly examined by a doctor who determines whether it is advisable for you to be prescribed the drug. Whether this actually happens is highly uncertain.

Health Which? carried out an investigation in June 2000 to find out whether appropriate safeguards were in place when 'lifestyle' drugs such as Viagra and Xenical were supplied over the Internet.

The study aimed to establish whether the drugs were being supplied to people for whom they were not suitable or in some cases even dangerous. It concluded that too many sites supplied drugs when, for medical reasons, they should not have. They also found that most of the sites that did not supply the drug made little or no effort to explain why the drug was not suitable for the patient.

You have to approach buying medicines over the Internet with great caution. You cannot be sure that the online doctors are qualified or that they have enough relevant information to make a valid diagnosis and prescribe appropriate drugs. Being prescribed a drug based purely on a questionnaire can most definitely pose health risks.

You also need to bear in mind that licensing requirements differ from one country to another. If you use a site based outside the UK you may be prescribed drugs that are not licensed in the UK. Drugs are also often sold under different brand names so it is difficult to know exactly what you have been prescribed.

Chapter 16

Careers

For those looking for a career change or a job move, the Internet can provide details of thousands of opportunities, categorised by both area of the country and profession. To help you secure a new job, the Internet can provide advice and ideas for updating your CV and perfecting your interview technique.

Online recruitment

If you are looking for a new job, the Internet is certainly your best starting point. According to a study in 2002 by the Cranfield School of Management, more than half of all UK-based organisations use the Internet for recruitment. This compares with just 17 per cent in 1999. The study also indicates that organisations are moving away from using online recruitment agencies and are choosing to advertise vacancies through their own sites, presumably owing to the cost of using an agency. So if you are looking for a job, use recruitment sites but also take at look at the websites of organisations that you would like to work for, and those of newspapers that advertise jobs.

Online recruitment agencies

There are hundreds of recruitment agencies with an online presence, some offering a full range of jobs and others specialising in niche markets. The majority are free of charge for the job searcher: they make their money by charging a commission to the employer. It pays to be registered with a few different agencies and if possible sign up to be sent details of jobs that fit your specification as and when they come in. The following are just a few examples of the better-known sites.

Hot Recruit (*www.hotrecruit.co.uk*) offers thousands of national and international jobs from the routine to the unusual. The site covers both the UK and continental Europe and sends job alerts by email when they come up. The site was initially designed for students and travellers but has been expanded to accommodate a wider range of opportunities for those under 35. Despite its growth, the site still manages to maintain its edge for the unusual.

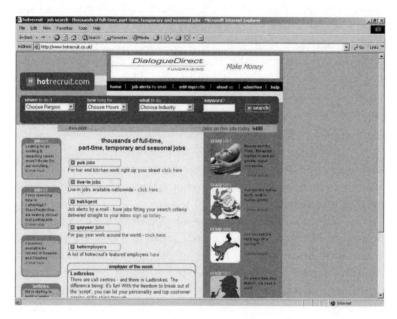

The Monster (*www.monster.co.uk*) recruitment site offers over a million job opportunities worldwide. The thing that makes this site stand out from the rest is the 'Create your CV' online option. This is a step-by-step guide to the CV writing process. The site has a friendly layout with the useful addition of a career centre that gives advice on interview techniques and negotiating salaries.

The Fifty On site (*www.fiftyon.co.uk*) is dedicated to those aged 50 and over. As well as vacancies it provides a regular online newsletter. Another excellent site for older jobseekers is the government's Age Positive Campaign website, *www.agepositive.gov.uk*.

Summer Jobs 4 Students (*www.summerjobs4students.co.uk*) is a comprehensive online directory of UK summer employment opportunities for young people attending colleges and universities. It provides details of temporary jobs throughout the UK covering a wide area of employment opportunities including tourism, leisure, hospitality, childcare, retail, agricultural as well as office jobs.

Reed (*www.reed.co.uk*) is one of the better-known 'bricks and mortar' recruitment agencies that now has an online presence. It takes about ten minutes to register on this vast site, but then, with more than 86,000 jobs to choose from, it is probably worth the effort. You can search on location, salary and job type, and use advanced search options to narrow the field. The site will provide email or text alerts if jobs come in matching your specifications.

There are some specialist sites for graduates. *Doctorjob.co.uk* and *grb.uk.com* are two of the best known. The prospects website (*www.prospects.ac.uk*) contains job vacancies and a facility for job-seeking graduates to put their CVs online.

Careers advice

If you are just starting out in the job market or you have reached a crossroads in your career, the Internet can provide help and advice on planning the way forward.

The majority of sites providing job opportunities also have sections that offer careers advice as well as practical help with securing a new job. There are also plenty of other sites that specialise in career guidance. To find a range, use a search engine to search on the keywords 'careers advice'. Alternatively, Careers A–Z (*www.careersa-z.co.uk*) is a good starting point. This is a free and independent website developed and maintained by the Topaz Partnership, a small group of specialists in education, IT and careers. For links to a whole range of resources, try Support 4 Learning (*www.support4learning.org.uk*). This is a directory site that has links to organisations that can help you move your career forward. Work Thing (*www.workthing.com*), a Guardian Media Group company, also provides well-presented careers information in addition to a job-search option. Those aged 19 and under will find helpful careers advice and information on the government's Connexions service website (*www.connexions-direct.com*).

New graduates are catered for at *www.prospects.ac.uk*, which covers careers information, advice on how to make decisions, help with applications, information on what jobs graduates have entered and many other topics. Another useful site is *www.gradunet.co.uk*. It provides careers advice as well as help with producing a stunning CV. If you are returning to employment, try the Department for Education and Skills (*www.dfes.gov.uk*) website. This site also caters for the retired, adults with special needs and those recently arrived from overseas. Those based in Scotland may like to try *www.scottish-enterprise.com* or *www.careers-scotland.org.uk*. Both sites provide advice on changing careers, finding a job and training.

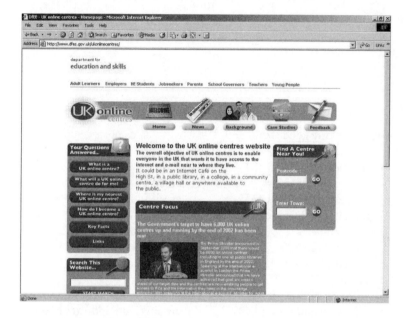

The Learndirect futures section (*www.learndirect-futures.co.uk*) provides advice on how to take charge of your career. There are options to match your skills and interests to opportunities in the workplace as well as advice on how to make the right choices either using online tools or with the support of career advisors.

Index